Finding Your
GOD-GIVEN PARTNER

A Dating & Relationship Guide

Thank you for being part of a successful book launch!! Enjoy reading!!

Funke Oladele

Finding Your
GOD-GIVEN
PARTNER
A Dating & Relationship Guide

Copyright © 2022 Funke Oladele

Published by:

Scripture quotations are taken from the Holy Bible, New International Version®, NIV®. Copyright © 1973, 1978, 1984, 2011 by Biblica, Inc.™ Used by permission of Zondervan. All rights reserved worldwide. www.zondervan.com The "NIV" and "New International Version" are trademarks registered in the United States Patent and Trademark Office by Biblica, Inc.™

Publishing Support Services:
PowerPoints4Living, LLC
info@powerpoints4living.com

Book Cover Design: Unique Graphic
Uniquegraphic200@gmail.com

Author Image: Dominion Perfect Images
https://www.dominionperfectimages.com/

Chapter Images:
Illustration 36769825 / Heart © Natalia Artemjeva |
Dreamstime.com;
Photo 114642470 / Compass Map © Ievgenii
Tryfonov | Dreamstime.com

ISBN: 979-8-218-06191-3

Printed in the United States of America
Independently Published

DEDICATION

I dedicate this book to my God-given and God-ordained husband, the one I spent a season of my life waiting for, the one I would've missed had not God hit the reset button on my life. I am forever grateful to God for aligning me with His will for my life.

ACKNOWLEDGMENTS

I would like to specially thank my editorial and production team, editors, Olubunmi Akindebe, Margaret Beasley, Emeka Iwuchukwu, and Elizabeth Akinrinsola for contributing to the successful publishing of this book.

I would like to acknowledge my children, Araoluwa and Lolade Oladele, who inspire me as I wrote this book and thought about when they would need it later in life.

I acknowledge the single youth ministry I worked with for many years. They also inspired me to write this book.

Finally, I would like to acknowledge my parents who have been married for nearly 35 years as of this writing for giving me a good foundation on love and marriage.

PREFACE

I give thanks to the Almighty God for giving me the opportunity to finally publish my first book. I remember reading the story book titled, *Ralia the Sugar Girl*, in the third grade in Nigeria, and I fantasized about the idea of writing a book at some point in the future. This desire increased as I grew into my teenage years, and I became determined to write about life experiences that could help guide other people. Back then, I had plotted out my life and pre-written my fairytale story of going through life without any problems, and even meeting my Prince Charming—whom, by the way, I fantasized so much about as a young girl that I often drew him as a tall, fine young man with well sculpted biceps and with a short but nicely shaped mohawk afro. I always drew his profile and carefully defined the features of his face with his nose perfectly fitting his oblong-shaped face and mouth drawn in proportion to his pointy nose. Our love story had been prewritten in my head and living happily ever after was the climax without thinking of the in-betweens. If only life was that linear and smooth, wouldn't the world be a perfect place?

I was born into a family of seven with me being the first of five beautiful girls. In other words, I have always been the guinea pig who had to figure things out first, learn, make mistakes, and then teach my sisters what to do and not to do. Sometimes, I came off a bit strong in my approach to teach my sisters, especially whenever I felt one was making the wrong decision. I could not, and still can't, stand watching someone fall into a ditch. Extending beyond my immediate family, the big sister and mentorship mindset always pushed me to teach, impart knowledge, advise, mentor, and encourage others to make wise decisions and be the best version of themselves.

I have also been blessed and privileged to serve as the leader of a youth and young adult group for more than seven years. I am passionate about teenagers and young adults because this is typically the life-phase where major decisions that impact their lives are made. I believe this delicate phase of life requires careful guidance and support. The average teenager thinks they are smart enough not to need advice from anyone. Also, many young adults become very excited about becoming adults and exercising their freedom from parental constraints, thereby taking risks and making decisions sometimes without carefully weighing the consequences. As I journey through life, I have come to learn that there are unspoken rules and societal expectations that people use to guide their lives and the decisions they make. These decisions can either make or break them.

As a young Christian, I gave my life to Christ around thirteen years of age, when I believed I had come of age to take the responsibility of building my faith and developing my relationship with Christ. At that age also, some of my classmates had boyfriends, and of course, some of the boys were starting to show interest in me. I was in secondary school in Nigeria, which is equivalent to 10th grade in high school in the United States. Thank God, I was in an all-girls boarding school, which I believe kept me somewhat away from the distraction of boys during school sessions. However, they would always make attempts to get my attention whenever I was home for the holidays. To be honest, it felt good getting all that attention from boys. In my teenage mind, at the time, it felt like validation of my femininity. However, I was so deep into God that I found it even more amusing to tell them off with an emphatic, "No." To them, it might have looked like I was playing hard to get, but to me, I was sold out for God. While I had a few guy friends whom I grew up with and had gotten close with, I was very clear about boundaries. I had promised God at a tender age that I would live my life for Him, not compromise my love for Him, and I would wait patiently for my future Mr. Right.

And so, life began. I have found myself in wrong relationships, following worldly standards of dating instead of God's standard, trying to help God write my love story, and I have observed good and not so good relationships around me. I have also been privileged by the sheer grace of God to be redirected by His leading to align with His purpose for my marital destiny, and I am ever grateful to Him for being so loving and faithful. In a place of surrender and total trust in Him, He divinely connected my husband and me together, establishing a beautiful union with a heavenly mandate.

Dear single Christian, I admonish you in the name of God, according to the Word of God in Romans 12:1, "And do not be conformed to this world, but be transformed by the renewing of your mind, so that you may prove what the will of God is, that which is good and acceptable and perfect."

I wrote this book to provide guidance as God directed me, based on biblical guidelines, inspiration of the Holy Spirit, personal experiences, and observation of other people's experiences. This book hopefully will open your eyes to the reality of the world we live in, to warn you of the dangers and consequences of going with the way of the world, and to lay out a step-by-step guide that will help you find your path to meeting your God-ordained partner.

Far too often, I have seen people struggle while dating and even later in their marriage, but the major source of the problems was created in their singleness. Some of these problems are due to a lack of adequate preparation, incorrect perception of what a relationship should be, unrealistic expectations, and many more misconceptions. For example, a person gets married with the expectation that it will always be a bed of roses and their needs will always be met. Anything short of that expectation becomes a problem because the person has not properly prepared for the good, bad, and ugly in marriage. The consequences of such are much greater than the benefit. Moreso, for Christians, you might find yourself in a dichotomic situation where you are confused about how to approach dating God's way or whether you should take the world's easy way.

This book serves as a step-by-step guide for godly relationships and finding your God-given partner as I believe in the efficacy and potency of the Word of God. I strongly believe that if you align yourself, your thoughts, and faith with His will and trust in the Lord, He will give you the desires of your heart and bring you to an expected end (Psalm 37:5 and Jeremiah 29:11).

Below are critical questions I would like to ask you to ponder as you read this book. Your answers to these questions will determine how much you gain from this book, help you assess your thought process, and gauge your level of trust in God being involved in finding your life partner:

> Do you believe God ordains who you are going to marry?

> Do you believe God can help you discover or find your life partner?

> Do you believe your decisions can make you miss your God-ordained partner?

The chapters in this book lay down a step-by-step guide to finding your God-given partner. Please note that I will be using the terms "God-ordained partner" and "God-given partner" interchangeably throughout this book. As you read through these chapters and reflect on your dating and relationship experience, you might discover that you've skipped some steps in your process. Please know that it is not too late to start over, even if you are in a relationship.

Starting over for some might mean discontinuing a current relationship, while for others, it simply means hitting the reset button to follow the steps laid out in this book and let God work out His purpose concerning you. I would advise that you read this book with an open mind and let the Holy Spirit do the work of transforming your mind in applying the points to your life. There are questions included in each chapter for self-reflection and planning for making improvements in preparation for your God-given partner and relationship.

CONTENTS

CHAPTER ONE
What is Dating and Why Date?

There is always a starting point to almost anything in life, and before any step is taken, there is need for preliminary work to ensure you have proper guidance, the right motivation, and the right mindset. Therefore, before moving forward, you should ask, what am I doing and why am I doing this? As you prepare to date or continue in a dating relationship, ask yourself why you want to date. This simple but loaded question will help you determine whether there is a reasonable need to date or not.

In many instances, dating is viewed as a societal norm or simply the next best thing to do at some stage of life. Unfortunately, this

> *Undefined relationships are not going to lead anywhere but a dead end.*

perspective has resulted in people dating for no reason or for the wrong reasons at the wrong time. When this happens, the relationships end up being directionless flings, leaving people broken, disappointed, and trapped in a continuous and unpleasant cycle. Some common non-plausible reasons for dating are peer pressure, age, everyone else is doing it, and so on. Dating solely for those reasons is not good enough. Before ever considering dating, it is important to take time to find out what dating is about, how it fits into your life, its purpose at your stage of life, and what it requires of you. This chapter will break down what dating is, what a relationship is, and the distinction between both.

What Is Dating?

The best way to fully comprehend something is to understand what it is all about. It is important to get a full understanding of the concept of dating which helps provide more insight into the world of relationships. Starting off with the literal meaning of dating, the Merriam-Webster Dictionary defines it as "usually a romantic social meeting with someone."[1] This definition indicates that this is a social arrangement to meet, which indicates that it is an avenue to connect. What this definition means, in my interpretation, is that the dating phase is the "introductory or getting to know each other phase." It is important to make good use of that opportunity to get to know one another and determine if you are a good fit for each other.

In the human resource world, this is the "interview phase." What happens in an interview? You are looking for a job, you answer questions asked by the potential employer, and you obtain more information regarding the company and the position. This is

---

[1] Merriam-Webster. (n.d.). Date. In *Merriam-Webster.com dictionary*. Retrieved July 17, 2021, from https://www.merriam-webster.com/dictionary/date

because full details are often not provided in a job posting or maybe it is not clear enough to you. After the employer asks you questions, you ask your own questions to determine if that's the job you want. Finally, you wait to find out if you are hired.

The caveat is that, if you are desperate for just any job, you will take the job offer even after determining it isn't the best fit for you. Why do we do that? In most cases, they call it job security. Let's take this back to dating. Are you dating or looking to date for "dating security"? Dating security simply means you just want a boyfriend or girlfriend to avoid being single. Are you settling for less when you should be filtering out the unnecessary options that only hinder you from connecting with God's plan for your life?

Unfortunately, people get into relationships and then immediately assume roles of married couples or begin modeling marriages when they aren't in a marriage. While marriage might be the goal, it can be a highway to a dead end without clear communication and gradual steps taken to get there. The question then becomes: what steps should be taken? Let's take a moment to dive further into the definition of dating to get a clear understanding of the concept of dating.

Dating being defined as a romantic social meeting also shows that it involves two people who are possibly attracted to each other, or at least one person is interested if not both. The number one criterion for dating is meeting someone and feeling attracted to them. Let's pause here for a second and think through this. Please note that it takes effort to meet someone, but even when you do, it is altogether another thing to feel attracted to them. It is very possible to meet someone and not be attracted to them, and a major part of dating is getting to know a person enough to determine if there is something you are attracted to about him or her. The other side, of course, is if the other person is also attracted to you or not.

Ah ha! This probably has you on the edge of your seat. In truth, you know how you feel about someone, but you may get so caught up in how you feel that you forget to discover if they are also attracted to you. When only one person is attracted to the other, it will always be a struggle to balance things out. This leads to frustration, disappointment, and dissatisfaction in relationships.

There is often a misconception of attraction being only drawn to or stricken by physical appearance. This has led some people into resenting the actual person after getting to know them. Don't get trapped by looks. They can be deceptive, and the Bible warns against this in Proverbs 31:30 by saying, "Charm is deceptive, and beauty is fleeting, but a woman who fears the Lord is to be praised." Sadly, misplaced priorities and lack of knowledge of this concept leads a lot of people to praise beauty over personality, which is hugely influenced by the media and the world's view of beauty. This is one of many instances in the Bible where we are warned not to conform to the patterns of this world (Romans 12:1). I highlighted Romans 12:1 in my introduction as a major motivator to read through the pages of this book. Please, let it sound as a note of warning and a voice of reason to you as you make decisions regarding dating and relationships. Unfortunately, conforming to the patterns of the world have led many to miss out on God's beautiful plans for their lives.

Another point to note in the definition of dating is the setting up of the opportunity to meet up and spend time together. Creating an atmosphere that enables both parties to communicate and connect in order to become more familiar with each other is going to be beneficial. This can vary depending on the situations surrounding the two individuals, such as proximity and availability. For people who live close to each other, it might mean meeting up at a local restaurant, going to the movies, going to a fun place, all depending on their interest and preferences. For long distance relationships, this could mean spending time talking on the phone, sending emails, video chatting, and so on. The medium you use to communicate does not matter if you are getting to spend time together and you both feel connected and are comfortable with your mode of communication. Communication is very crucial to the sustainability of a relationship.

The purpose of spending time together is to gather information about the person that can be useful in making informed decisions as to whether you should get into a relationship with him or her. Such information includes sustained attraction to each other, compatibility, having good flowing conversations, understanding each other to some extent, and ability to relate well with one another. And finally, and most importantly, when making a decision after getting to know this person, the question to note is can you tolerate one another? Just because you are attracted to them, fantasize about that special person, desire a future with them does not mean you should. Such feelings are not enough reasons to proceed into a relationship with them. When I was single, I had decided after one or a few dates with some guys that I was not interested in them. In one instance, it was as a result of the way he was behaving, not respecting personal space. In another instance, it was lack of attraction or connection.

Therefore, it is advisable for you to assess the person you are dating after getting to know him or her for a period of time and make an informed decision. Dating should have an end; it shouldn't last for a long time. While I can't tell you exactly how long it should last, keep that analogy of an interview in your mind. Should you still be dating after three, four, five or six months? People commonly say you can make a decision after three dates, and some take two months; it all depends on the people involved. Nevertheless, when you get to the point where you've gotten to know the person to some extent and trust that their "resume" or what you know about them is sufficient enough to make a decision, ask yourself these questions below:

➤ Does being with this person bring me joy most of the time?

➤ Am I at peace when I have conversations with this person?

➤ Are we, as a couple, able to resolve conflicts when they arise?

➤ Do I like the way the person relates with other people?

➤ Does this person think reasonably?

➤ What can't I stand about this person?

You can also include any other questions in your mind that align with you and your values.

One of the most misleading things in our world today is the way people confuse dating, courtship, and relationships. You rarely ever hear the word "courtship" or "courting." But it is an important word to know and even work toward. I will break this down in a way you can understand. Way too many words are being used around finding love and relationships that people keep looking for abstract things without the full knowledge of what they are looking for. The Bible emphasizes the importance of knowledge in many instances. Hosea 4:6 states, "My people perish for lack of knowledge."

Having gone through my late teens and 20s watching myself and others struggle to navigate the dating and relationship world, I realized the expedient need for a practical guide to dating and relationships. Nobody is born with a manual on this stuff. However, people with life experiences have an obligation to provide guidance for others going through similar situations. I believe human ideologies and idiosyncrasies are learned. However, not learning the right information can cause a lot of damage. I want to impact my world by sharing knowledge and bringing guidance, information, and resources that will help positively influence people to be the best version of themselves as I also work toward being the best version of myself.

In our world today, dating is sometimes misconstrued to mean being in a relationship or you might find people stuck in the dating stage for a long time. Being in a romantic relationship is not the same as dating. Wait a minute! You mean to tell me that all this time you have been using the words dating and relationship interchangeably, but they mean different things? If this is your thought at this point, you are not alone, and this is why we are exploring this together so you can start getting the right mindset, the right information, and the right guidance.

Once we go through what dating is, we will delve into the world of relationships to learn what it's all about. In a nutshell, dating is a prelude to a courting relationship, and the outcome of dating determines the existence of a courtship or official relationship as we typically call it. If you've successfully met someone and you are attracted to each other and can stand each other, then you agree to go into a relationship or courtship together. So, what is a relationship? We will explore this in the next section of this chapter.

What Is a Relationship?

A relationship is simply defined as a state of being related or interrelated. According to the Merriam Webster Dictionary, a relationship is a connection, association, or involvement.[2] What does this mean? It is the condition or place of being united. Considering the previous definition of dating, for a relationship to happen, there should've been an assessment period, a determination made, and an agreement between both parties to make it a relationship. This, then, is the beginning of a walk together or a union.

We can acknowledge that there are different kinds of relationships. A platonic friendship is a kind of relationship, so is a family relationship, a religious relationship, a professional relationship, and so on. It is plausible to conclude that each of these relationships require different approaches and are unique in nature. A father-daughter relationship is different from a pastor-to-member relationship and from a boyfriend-girlfriend relationship. Understanding the unique nature of your relationship helps to take a unique approach toward it. Let me also say that a non-Christian boyfriend-girlfriend relationship is different from a Christian boyfriend-girlfriend relationship.

> In a courtship, two people have a clear agreement to develop the relationship into marriage someday.

---

[2] Merriam-Webster. (n.d.). Relationship. In *Merriam-Webster.com dictionary*. Retrieved December 10, 2021, from https://www.merriam-webster.com/dictionary/relationship

As you can deduce from the definition of dating, being in a relationship means you are taking things a step further. Basically, this can be described as moving from a first meeting to deciding if you get along enough to go beyond the platonic stage. The relationship stage is where you get to know each other beyond the surface level and agree that you are working together toward marriage, which is simply the definition of courtship.

In a courtship, two people have a clear agreement to develop the relationship into marriage someday. Courtship is what every single Christian should aim for rather than having an undefined relationship without goals, aims, or objectives. Undefined relationships lead to a dead end.

As you reflect on these definitions, let them serve as a way to assess your views and how you want to improve it through better enlightenment to work toward developing healthier and more focused relationships. The ultimate goal is to build relationships that bring glory to God.

I hereby encourage you to be ready to grasp the revelation the Holy Spirit has in store for you in this book. Having taken time to get a better understanding of what dating is and a relationship is, the remaining chapters of this book will focus on what to consider, keep in perspective, do, and avoid in the dating and courting relationship or the courtship phase. It will also focus on how to progress through the different phases leading up to marriage.

Chapter One Questions

1. What has been your perspective about dating?

2. In your opinion, what's the difference between dating and courtship?

3. Have you been misinterpreting dating all this time?

4. How has this chapter improved your understanding of dating?

5. What is most important to you about dating?

6. What are your thoughts about courtship which is most commonly referred to as being in a relationship?

7. What approach will you start taking toward dating now?

CHAPTER TWO
The Preparation Phase
Before Thinking about Dating

The dating and relationship world can be so complicated that it becomes easy for anyone to lose themselves in the process without proper orientation and guidance. As a single Christian, I knew it was important to involve God in anything I did, but it wasn't clear to me to what extent I needed to involve Him in my dating and relationship life. The depth of this preparation phase was quite absent in my single days and in the failed relationships I had prior to meeting my husband. However, God made sure I had that time with Him to encounter Him more, to discover myself better, and to

Therefore, I identify this preparation phase as the most important phase leading toward starting and building a successful godly relationship.

seek His will and direction for my marital life in the months leading to meeting my husband.

1. Start with God

It is important to follow a step-by-step process in unfolding a relationship so that it becomes worthwhile and to ensure you are carefully making a Spirit-guided decision. It's always easy to make decisions based on how we feel. It is also easy to meet people sometimes, but problems arise when you can't seem to understand each other.

Therefore, the first phase before dating is the preparation phase. This is the foundational phase, and it starts with God. The foundational phase has been illustrated in Psalm 127:1 which states, "Unless the Lord builds the house, they labor in vain, who build it; Unless the Lord guards the city, the watchman stays awake in vain." This is to show you that God is the principal builder needed in your foundation.

There is nothing more beautiful, innovative, and brilliant than the story of creation. The older I get the more I see more clearly that God is the beginning and the end of all things. Let's take a look at Genesis 1 to understand this concept, starting from verse 1:

> *[1] In the beginning, God created the heavens and the earth. [2] Now the earth was formless and empty, darkness was over the surface of the deep, and the Spirit of God was hovering over the waters. [3] And God said, "Let there be light," and there was light."*

And so, the story of creation continued. This story paints a picture of God stepping in *before* the world came into existence. God was the Initiator. He was the Orchestrator. He saw the earth without form and made a masterpiece out of it. If you want a beautiful masterpiece, just hand that blank slate to the Master Planner. This revelation will save you both heartache and time in trying to figure it out all by yourself.

We often make the mistake of doing things based on our needs and feelings, with the just-go-for-it mindset. What happens when you just jump into a car without any idea where you're going, no GPS or compass, and simply driving in a random direction? You will only go so far as your money to buy gas lasts and still be nowhere. Verse 2 and 3 of Genesis 1 reveals that there was darkness and then God said, "Let there be light," and there was light. Anything we embark on without God's involvement is baseless and indicates we are walking in darkness. There will never be clear direction in darkness, there is no fulfillment in darkness, and it makes it difficult to identify a definite destination. I pray for you as you read this book and apply these principles to your life that the Lord will illuminate your world and dispel every form of darkness hovering over your marital destiny.

The presence of God always makes a difference in everything we do as His beloved children. Therefore, I identify this preparation phase as the most important phase that leads toward starting and building a successful godly relationship in marriage. As a Christian, building a relationship with God is very crucial to living a fulfilling life, which includes long-lasting and successful relationships with others.

This is evident in Matthew 22, when an expert in the law asked the question, "What is the greatest commandment?"

In verse 37, Jesus replied, "Love the Lord your God with all your heart and with all your soul and with all your mind. This is the first and greatest commandment. And the second is like it: Love your neighbor as yourself."

This shows the importance of falling in love with God first, giving yourself to Him, knowing Him more, and giving your time and all to love and serve Him. This, in and of itself, is enough to keep you occupied. The Holy Spirit revealed to me, as I wrote this line, that this phase is a learning ground for the relationship you desire. If you read over verse 37, you'll see how loving the Lord with all your heart, soul, and mind should be the basis for a relationship with a Christian of the opposite sex. And if you both do this, then neither of you will ever have problems loving each other with your whole beings. Thank you, Holy Spirit, for this revelation. Dear brother or sister reading this book, did you catch that? The fine print, template, and model for the relationship you desire lies in and depends on how strong and deep your relationship with God is.

> The number one prerequisite to a failed relationship is the absence of God in the foundation of the relationship.

Unfortunately, the costliest mistake many of us tend to make is to start with everything else but God. Perhaps you think dating has nothing to do with spirituality. Google is usually a popular source of information that many people start with, including me, or we would ask our friends. Let's take a closer look at why you should start with God as the foundation for your future dating and marriage relationships. We'll examine the Bible. The following scriptures highlight why you should start with God.

God Is the Creator

Genesis 1:27 – *So God created mankind in his own image, in the image of God he created them; male and female he created them.*

This verse indicates that God created you with His own identity and with your compatible partner of the opposite sex in mind. He had a plan in mind at the beginning and has perfected it all, but we must walk in His way, according to His leading to actualize what He has already established

John 1:2-3 – *He was with God in the beginning. Through him all things were made; without him nothing was made that has been made.*

This Bible text indicates that you are a reflection of God, meaning He knows you to the depth of your being, and the things you do not understand about yourself are well known to him. Due to the fact that God is the beginning and the end of all things, you must always go back to Him. Stay connected to Him to strengthen that identity and relationship.

God Expects You to Commit Your Desires and Plans to Him

Proverbs 3:6 – *In all your ways submit to him, and he will make your paths straight.*

Psalm 37:4-5 – *⁴ Delight thyself also in the Lord: and he shall give thee the desires of thine heart. ⁵ Commit thy way unto the Lord; trust also in him; and he shall bring it to pass.*

If you pay close attention to the scriptures listed above, they each have conditions, instructions, and an outcome, which means there are consequences if you do otherwise to the commanded course of action. These texts command you to commit your plans to Him before you embark on the journey or take any steps, and if you do, then He will make your path straight. Therefore, the number one prerequisite to a failed relationship is the absence of God in the foundation of the relationship. I encourage you to be in total surrender to God, prioritizing Him, trusting that He knows what you need and will supply it all according to his riches in glory.

God Is Love

> **1 John 4:16** – *And we have known and believed the love that God has for us. God is love, and he who abides in love abides in God, and God in him.*

Finally, if none of the other Bible texts resonate with you, I hope to drive the point home with the keyword "love." If love was all you needed in a relationship, then guess what? God is love! He embodies all you desire. He is the love you seek to find in humans who will never satisfy your soul. I hereby emphasize that you start by getting involved with Love (God). No human can ever truly love or feel loved in return unless they've experienced God. I plead with you to fall in love with Love (God) and let Him overwhelm you, let Him be your standard, and let Him be all that you see.

Also, have you ever seen any love as great as the love of God on earth? I mean, for a human being to sacrifice his only son for the sake of others? Have you seen any human who can love so greatly that they forgive all your sins no matter how wicked they are? I haven't seen or heard of such a person or people. The Bible provides the answer, stating, "Greater love has no one than this, than to lay down one's life for his friends" (John 15:13). I, therefore, present to you "Love" in the purest form. The Love that calls light out of darkness, that made the universe out of nothing, that made humans in His own image, that breathed His breath into us, gave us all a purpose and a will, provides a means of redemption by sacrificing His only begotten Son so that we may have life in abundance. Why will you have it any other way? It will do you much good to get lost in the world of the love of God, truly connect with God, and learn more about Him so that you may embody His love. Please save yourself the trouble and heartache and let Him perfect all that concerns you (Psalm 138:8).

Because I was a devoted Christian, actively involved in church activities as a single woman, I thought I had involved God when I started dating. I was quick to turn down guys I didn't like and then prayed for a sign when I found one I liked. However, now in retrospect, I realize I could've developed a deeper relationship with God to be the model for the relationship I desired. If I had a clear understanding of the importance of the role of God in my singleness, dating, and relationships, I would have surrendered that aspect of my life to Him earlier. Even though I prayed when I met a potential date, I may have made my conclusion based on what I thought were signs from God but were probably more based on self-conviction than God's direction. Making self-gratifying decisions in the moment without proper connection with and direction from God can create a gap that will not be quite satisfying in the long run.

2. Love and Develop Yourself

Define Your Identity

Defining your identity enables you to stay deeply rooted. What does that mean? People have different sources that have become the foundation of their existence. However, as a Christian, your identity must be established and deeply rooted in Christ. Jesus gave an illustration that explains this more clearly in John 15:5, saying, "I am the vine; you are the branches. If you remain in me and I in you, you will bear much fruit; apart from me you can do nothing."

Let's dissect this Bible verse, starting with the vine. What is a vine? According to the Merriam-Webster Dictionary, a "vine is a plant whose stem requires support, and which climbs by tendrils or twining or creeps along the ground.[3]" You can view this vine as the source which grows and sprouts with branches that represent us where the vine is Christ. Those branches are expected to bear fruit. The fruit you bear is your identity, your personality, and what people see in you. This is confirmed in Matthew 7:20, which states, "Wherefore by their fruits ye shall know them."

Being deeply rooted also means that a lot of investment has gone into you, including your upbringing and your cultural and spiritual values. You must be able to embrace yourself, be submissive to learn, and undergo a pruning, taming, and grooming process that takes place, in most cases, under your parents' or guardians' guidance. Parents are the first guides we get in life, teaching us to differentiate what is right from wrong…if you are privileged enough to have such spiritual parents. Disobeying your parents and following after your heart's desires, especially in the area of love, can spell doom. For example, if you are a teenager and you decide to start sneaking out of the house to meet up with your boyfriend or girlfriend, then you are on a highway to a cycle of sin. It is also dangerous because something bad can happen to you while you are out, such as getting into an accident or being kidnaped.

I must admit that not everyone has the opportunity to have good parenting which emphasizes Christian principles and good moral teaching. In such cases, these might create a challenge in the fruits produced, such as one's personality, behaviors, and so on. I do however believe that, once a person comes to the full knowledge of

---

[3] "Vine." *Merriam-Webster.com Dictionary*, Merriam-Webster, https://www.merriam-webster.com/dictionary/vine. Accessed 20 Dec. 2021.

Christ and follows biblical guidelines, he or she carries the full identity of Christ and becomes rooted in Him.

Defining one's identity seems to be very difficult for people, because there are so many expectations at different ages. For example, among high school kids, there are issues with social pressure which leads to identity crisis, which causes people to become involved in things they wouldn't normally choose to do on their own. Other examples are people giving in to the pressure to have sex at a certain age or to do drugs and other ungodly things.

I therefore urge you to spend time to solidify your identity in Christ. Identify your values by asking yourself the following questions:

➤ What do I stand for?

➤ What can't I compromise on?

➤ What would I like to be known as?

➤ What behaviors/attitude will help me attain that true picture of myself?

Finally, be a true Christian in thoughts, words, and deeds, whether you are inside or outside of church. Be consistent with your personality and not give mixed signals about yourself. Know what you stand for and stand by it. I am a believer in the saying by Alexander Hamilton, "If you don't stand for something, you will fall for anything." This means, when your identity is not deeply rooted, you will be confused and easily deceived.

Establish Your Purpose in Life (What Are Your Goals)
Establishing your purpose is another key step in knowing and developing yourself. I will provide two examples of biblical characters who identified their purpose.

The first is David. He spent years in his father's field tending to sheep, and in this work, his purpose was born, skills developed, and his destiny launched. He took time to care for, provide food, protect, and defend his father's sheep. This was the time he invested in himself and developed his leadership skills. So how does taking care of sheep equate with leading people? The answer can be found in Colossians 3:23, which states, "Whatever you do, work at it with all your heart, as working for the Lord, not for human masters." God has a way of working His purpose out in whatever you do and glorifies Himself through it all. He has a way of testing you and observing the way you handle seemingly small tasks before He decides to call you to greater ones.

The second biblical example is Esther, the beautiful, smart, visionary, young orphan who was raised by her older cousin, Mordecai. She recognized the need of her people and decided to find a way to save them as a queen. She used her wisdom to lead a whole race of people out of destruction and oppression (Esther 2-5).

Dear reader, please recognize that building yourself and finding your purpose is the basis for how far you will go in life. You probably thought this was only going to be about finding love and a happily-ever-after, right? Well, it is, but note that these steps are precursors to finding your life partner. Combining all these factors will lead to finding fulfillment in life. Identifying your purpose provides a sense of direction in every aspect of life, including love and marriage.

Invest in Yourself and Set Timelines
In some cases, ladies tend to be ready to marry earlier than men. I am not here to give you a timeline for getting married, but part of knowing yourself and your purpose is setting goals and projected timelines (e.g., graduating college at a certain age, getting a job,

getting married). You may not achieve it exactly the way you projected, but it won't be too far off.

While priorities may vary by individual, it is important to set your priorities right. Traditionally, most men are inclined to achieve a lot first with the intention of being financially stable. Marriage is usually at the bottom of their list. On the other hand, most ladies prioritize their personal achievements and marriage simultaneously. Some women prioritize marriage first. Though the times are changing with both men and women, and now most focus on personal achievements first, such as education and career, with the thought of marriage coming later.

My goal is not to judge what is right or wrong but to provide guidance and insight for your consideration. It is important to have your personal life goals established and be determined to achieve them. This is applicable to men and women. However, while setting timelines, please do not place the thought of marriage or finding a life partner on the back burner, because you might miss a great opportunity to find the person of your dreams.

The danger in putting marriage off till later might make it more difficult to get what they are looking for and might end up going with whoever they find. Does this mean you can miss your God-given partner? I believe so! The saying, "Make hay while the sun shines," is very true, and the biblical version of this is found in Ecclesiastes 3:1, which says, "There is a time for everything, and a season for every activity under the heavens."

If you give it a thought, you will realize that even the story of creation had a timeline. Create order and a sense of direction in your life and watch God bring all your plans to fruition. Get organized and plan out your life. I would like to reveal to you the secret of the way God works. He created you in His own image and breathed into you life. Therefore, He knows you can think

21

similarly and create things similarly. That's why He gave humans the power to dominate and subdue the earth. He expects us to make decisions, be able to plan, desire, envision, and He works on those things to bring them to life. Jeremiah 29:11 shows that God makes plans and functions on plans. Proverbs 16:3 says, "Commit to the Lord whatever you do, and he will establish your plans." This confirms that God's power thrives where there is a plan.

Finally, in Habakkuk 2:2-3, God gave instructions: "Write down the revelation and make it plain on a tablet so that a herald may run with it. For the revelation awaits an appointed time; it speaks of the end and will not prove false. Though it lingers, wait for it; it will certainly come and will not delay." This Bible text is as potent and powerful as it sounds. Just try God and see. Take a bold step of faith today and write out your plans by setting a timeline to it.

> You cannot conform God and the person you will marry to fit into your plan and timeline, but you can let God merge your will, goals, and plan with His.

I remember having a mental timeline when I was younger and now, I realize, I've always been a planner. As I progressed in my education track, I was able to set a predictable timeline as stated below:

➢ Graduate from College at age 21

➢ Complete masters at age 23/24

➢ Get married at age 25

This timeline was a driving force, challenging me to work toward achieving these goals. I needed to accomplish them at the set time. I confess to you, it wasn't easy. There were days of tears, sweat, heartbreaks, and breakups before achieving these goals in God's time. Yes, I said God's time, because His ways are not our ways, and His timeline is not exactly our timeline. However, He gives us our heart's desires, and as stated in Habakkuk 2:3, "Though it lingers, wait for it." Did I surrender to God easily? No! I wanted to make it happen. I wanted to meet my timeline. I tried hard to help God fill in the blanks, and I ended up being humbled by God to a place of surrender.

Getting your life partner is different from getting a college degree, because you are not in full control of the process. There are two other entities involved, and it requires a completely different approach to achieve this goal. You cannot conform God and the person you will marry to fit into your plan and timeline, but you can let God merge your will, goals, and plan with His.

In reality, God answered my prayers or granted these requests in the following order:

➢ Graduated with a bachelor's degree at age 21

➢ Obtained master's degree at age 26

➢ Got married at age 28

Once you set your goals, present them to the Lord, and let Him bring them to pass. "Do not be anxious about anything, but in every situation, by prayer and petition, with thanksgiving, present your requests to God" (Philippians 4:6). Don't let your timeline rob you of the opportunity to enjoy God's best at His chosen time. Be open-minded and flexible while submitting yourself to God, allowing Him to work out His own purpose in your life.

3. Work on Yourself (Physical Appearance, Attitude, and Conduct)

While you might be convinced that you have everything together, it is important for you to be honest with yourself and identify your weaknesses. The truth is that we are all a work in progress, and we must never stop working on ourselves.

I encourage you to do this small exercise of looking at yourself in the mirror, assess yourself deeply, and ask this simple question, "Would you date you?" You'll probably quickly answer with a big yes without giving it a second thought. In reality, the person you are looking for also has things they are looking for in a potential partner just as you do. This is the time to prepare yourself for what you are praying for so that you don't get caught off guard.

There is a humorously common statement single people say about looking your best everywhere you go because you never know where you'll meet "the one." This saying is very true, but it's not only applicable to physical appearance. This idea should include everything about you, your attitude, your physical appearance, and the way you relate with others. People meet in the most unlikely places and situations, and there is usually something endearing about the person before getting to know them more. For example, some people are attracted to someone they meet at a train station, at a restaurant just eating, or at a party, and so on. The attraction could be the way the person carries themselves, relates with other people, the way they smile, the way they eat, and so forth.

Physical appearance really *does* matter, whether for male or female, but it's not the only factor to consider. People see you first before getting to know your personality, so do what you can to look good to your level of comfort. I would also like to challenge you to ask yourself: what does your way of life and appearance portray about you? This will lead to the next point.

Who Are You Attracting and Are They Your Ideal Partner?
The dating world is like an open market: display your product and make it appealing to your targeted customer. For example, if you are interviewing for a corporate job, you would need to dress business casual or formal depending on the setting, and if you are going to get a job as a painter, you need to get the appropriate casual clothing for it.

Ask yourself this question: what kind of man or woman do I want? Then position yourself to be marketable to such. Yes, I used the word *marketable* because the other person you are trying to attract is also in the market...looking. You will attract your targeted audience.

While you are waiting for your perfect match, please work on yourself so you can also be a perfect fit for him or her. It is great to be yourself and not pretend to be someone you are not, but if you know there are certain things you need to improve, I advise you take time to work on those things. Hear this: you shouldn't be looking for someone to complete you. Rather, you should work on making yourself whole and awesome by yourself. In doing this, meeting with another complete person helps you both to better complement each other.

Now that you understand why you should work on yourself and fall in love with yourself before dating, you should know the dangers of not having an identity. Without a proper identity rooted in values and foundation building, you can easily be swayed and become confused. It will be difficult for you to set proper boundaries or to determine what's good for you or not. You will find it easy to follow other people's paths without much direction or mind of your own. This will make it difficult for you to live a fulfilling life and can be detrimental to finding your God-given partner.

On the other hand, the benefits of working on yourself and developing your individuality far outweighs the negatives. Some of these benefits are as follows:

➢ You build a strong level of confidence to take on anything in life and achieve all you set your mind to.

➢ You will define your personal values that drive your life, decisions, and opinions.

➢ You will have a sense of direction and be able to identify your purpose in life.

➢ You have a standard, meaning you have things you will not compromise on and can make decisions unapologetically.

4. Establish Your Purpose for Dating (Why Are You Looking for a Relationship?)

Question: Why do you date?

If you are just getting started, why are you planning to date?

It is important to establish a reasonable purpose for dating because the motive behind dating contributes to the outcome of the relationship. This means that dating for the right reasons, with a purpose, sets the tone for a desired outcome. It keeps the two people in a relationship focused and in agreement.

There is a general misleading school of thought that dating is necessary once you reach a certain age. These days, kids in elementary school, middle school, and high school date because everyone is doing it. Unfortunately, there are adults who date without having any specific reason for doing so or without having the mental capacity for a relationship. Dating is for mature minds who have the intention of working toward marriage. Dating is not for fun. Dating is not like buying the same clothes your friends are wearing. It is a serious business that can lead to relationships that can impact your destiny and purpose either positively or negatively. The reason why teenage pregnancies occur is that young people who are typically not mentally and physically mature enough to date are finding themselves in situations that are beyond their capacity.

Similarly, adults who don't have any specific purpose for dating end up hurting other people and wasting their time. Indeed, dating in this way can lead to many unplanned situations, such as emotional abuse, neglect, and unplanned pregnancies. It is therefore advisable to date with a purpose at a mature age when you are equipped mentally, physically, and spiritually to handle it, especially when you are ready to let God have His way.

To establish your purpose for dating, keep the following things in mind:

Identify what you want in a potential partner based on your values (physical, attitude, religion, and status).

Make sure you are ready. You don't need to date or go into a romantic relationship if there is no specific purpose to eventually marry. Some people land themselves in relationships that should've been casual friendships. If you're not ready, just make friends with others.

Chapter Two Questions

1. Do you have a relationship with God?

2. How has your relationship with God been?

3. Have you sought God and loved Him before seeking humanly love?

4. What must you do before dating? There is a saying, "Which came first, the egg or the chicken?"

5. What do you need to improve about yourself and how do you plan to achieve this?

6. Do you have a timeline for your life's goals including when you hope to get married? If not, take time to do this and submit it God.

CHAPTER THREE
Searching and Waiting Phase

In the world of love and relationships, there are new words you should be familiar with: searching, spotting, positioning, and finding. You are probably wondering why I'm making the already complicated relationship sphere more difficult with new words. These words all have their meanings and purpose. In the grand scheme of things, God's original intent was for a man to find a wife as stated in Proverbs 18:22, "He who finds a wife, finds a good thing and obtains favor from the Lord." Call it archaic if you will, but it is the Word of God, and it never fails.

Regardless, it is logical to wonder if a woman should wait till eternity for a man to find her. This makes me remember a line of

God saw a need in Adam and decided to create that companion for him, hence the choice of words, God-given.

the hymn *Blessed Assurance*[4]. In verse two, it says, "Watching and waiting, looking above." This phrase is about waiting, but it is also about taking action while waiting. A lady is not expected to sit idle, complacent in her room, expecting to be found.

Let's study the classic example of Ruth in the book of Ruth. Ruth was a young widow who decided to follow her mother-in-law, Naomi, to her hometown after her husband died. Her priority was to take care of her mother-in-law, and so to get food, she started gleaning wheat in the fields. Eventually, her ability to stay focused while positioning herself in a place where she could be found led to her meeting Boaz, her God-given partner. Boaz took notice of her or spotted her and never let her out of his sight.

In this chapter, I will provide guidance about the role of God, man, and woman in discovering your God-given partner. You will learn how to know when you are ready for your God-given partner and the role of God, man, and woman in finding and connecting with that person.

I begin by taking you back to the beginning of Adam and Eve's love story in Genesis 2. The Lord God said, "*It is* not good that man should be alone; I will make him a helper comparable to him." God and Adam had a very close relationship, and as a result, God was able to identify this man's need for a human companion. The first lesson for both guys and ladies is to make sure you have that deep relationship with God, that is, to be so lost in God that He will meet your needs. The Bible says, "And my God will meet

---

[4] *Ancient and Modern: hymnas and songs for refreshing worship* 601
Text: Fanny Crosby, (Frances Jane vanAlstyne) (1820-1915)
Music (BLESSED ASSURANCE 9 1099 and refrain): Phoebe Palmer Knapp (1839-1908).

your needs according to the riches of his glory in Christ Jesus" (Philippians 4:19).

We tend to get so anxious about our needs…needs built on expectations of what should be done at a certain age or on selfish desires. God saw a need in Adam and knew that it was not good for Adam to be alone, though he was a perfectly made man. Adam was busy doing what God created him to do, tending to the Garden of Eden and building a relationship with God. So, I ask you, what do you spend most of your time doing? Assess yourself and decide to identify what God wants you to do. Find your purpose!

> It is here, in your singleness, that God shapes you for the future ahead of you.

Remember, as stated in the previous chapter, that it is important to know your purpose and walk in it.

After God identified that it is not good for man to be alone, He decided to make a helper suitable for Adam. So here you have it! God saw a need in Adam and decided to create that companion for him, hence the choice of words, "God-given." An important point to note here is that this conversation was going on between God and God alone. Adam was not involved.

I would like to pause here and quickly discuss how important it is to dedicate your singleness to God. It is here, in your singleness, that God shapes you for the future ahead of you. Many people see this phase of their life as a time to "mess around" with anybody they want—sow their wild oats so to speak. You know what that

31

means if that is you. It is a time where you are single but not always alone…there is always a guy or girl to keep you company. It is "friends with benefits."

But as long as you continue to mess around, God will not identify a need for a suitable partner for you. This will make you vulnerable to mistakes even to the point of choosing the wrong partner. I therefore plead with you in the name of Christ to desist from every ungodly companionship you've created for yourself—which mainly wastes your time, dissuades you from God's purpose for your life, and distracts you from connecting to God. Time wasters are always available, luring you by promising to meet a need in your life. There have been instances of people who dated for years eventually breaking up. I believe this is a classic example of being with a time waster. Indeed, they might even have concluded in the beginning that they were best for each other without God's involvement. It was a lie. A waste of time.

> **Proverbs 18:22** says, *"He who finds a wife finds a good thing and obtains favor from the lord."* It doesn't say, *"She who finds a husband…"*

Therefore, laying out the whole equation from this Bible verse about the role of God, we can deduce that the man does the searching and finding of a wife with the help of God, and when he does find her, he finds favor with God. This might make someone wonder what the role of the woman should be. God, who is impartial, is involved every step of the way in what a man or a woman does. He will also help in positioning the woman where she could be discovered by the man, who can then approach her, woo her, and make her his with the intention of marrying her. The woman then accepts the man whom God has identified, provided, and is now presenting her to. The story of Adam and Eve in Genesis 2 showed how deeply involved God was in their coming together. God went to work by putting Adam to sleep to create a woman who would fit His purpose and life. This He did without Adam's input or interruption (Genesis 2:21).

God made the woman from Adam's rib. Here comes the compatibility part. They had a similar and complementary build. Adam eventually "spotted" her after God "positioned" her where he could see her or find her. Adam was made to be the father of humankind and God created a woman who would walk that journey with Adam so that they could fulfill the purpose of God for their lives. Very often, I have seen eligible bachelors and bachelorettes struggle with connecting to their God-given partner due to their lack of knowledge of the role God has given them and thereby going for their self-sought partner for their self-gratifying purpose. I was also guilty of this.

This revelation made me realize that we can strive for something in vain because God has not identified the need and we have not surrendered to Him. Many men and ladies find themselves in dead-end, purposeless relationships because they were not made for each other. The message here for both men and women is to be in total surrender to God. Like Adam and Eve, wait on the Lord for the right time and He will make all things beautiful beyond your wildest imagination. Nevertheless, while you are waiting, you must align with God's purpose for yourself, maximize your potential, and dwell in His presence daily.

Often, there are men who date more than one lady at the same time without making any commitment to them. Alternatively, and just as bad, he will date someone for years without ending up in marriage only to turn around and marry some other woman after only a short period of dating. While some strategically keep multiple partners in order to choose the best one of the lot, there are also some who are sincerely in relationships for a long time, but the time spent was not the right time. Perhaps, it was not yet the right time in God's eyes. When God steps in and decides that it's time, He transforms the man, interrupts his routine, and changes his mind set by putting him to "sleep" like He did for Adam.

Then, when God is done molding Eve, He brings her before Adam and then they hit it off. The same also happens to women. Another example of this happening is couples who break up after dating for more than five years only to turn around and marry someone else within a year or two. In such scenarios, there is usually an emotional reaction to the amount of time that had been wasted in the previous relationship. The truth is that they were most likely not made for each other yet wasted each other's time despite loving each other.

The warning here for men and women is to avoid "messing around," "testing the waters," "having flings," or living without a purpose while waiting on God. You should be intentional about your singleness, being empowered and equipped with all the knowledge, tools, and wisdom you need for life and livelihood.

To the ladies, recognize that God carefully crafted you and equipped you with all you need to fit into His purpose for you and your future marriage. However, have you truly allowed God to mold you? Do you still need to surrender yourself to Him so that He can continue working on you and prepare you for your own Adam? To the men, God still works the same way He did with Adam. He knows exactly what you need and the desires of your heart. He knows when you need a companion, and He already has a plan in place for you. He swings into action when you commit it all into His hands, which is what happened when Adam was put to sleep.

Are you walking daily in His will? Are you letting Him breathe into you and fill you up with all the good virtues you need? If not, it's time to start. Walk with God, surrender yourself to Him, and let Him make you whole and miraculously connect you to your suitable partner. I, therefore, encourage you to take time to trust God to present you with what His purpose for your life is.

Prior to meeting my husband, I found myself in dead-end relationships, which I now clearly know were not God's purpose for my life. Unfortunately, I didn't know that at the time. However, when it was time to start marriage, God stepped in and worked out his purpose for my life. I remember meeting my husband. He said he had initially seen my picture and took note that he would like to know this girl, and

> You need to repent from writing your own love story and let God wow you with a well-crafted manuscript of your heavenly-orchestrated love story.

then he reached out to me. We eventually started communicating and given the fact that we were over 5,000 miles away from each other in different countries, there was no plan for us to meet each other. However, within a month of us getting to know each other, I found myself on a plane to his country due to a family obligation. God created a way to present me to this man. He then made his intention known to me.

We are in a day and age where the world has created some human guidelines and expectations for relationships and marriage. Dear brother or sister, unless you conform to God's original intent for marriage, it might be difficult to get divine direction about finding your God-given partner. Hence the reason for choosing to use the term God-given or God-ordained. You must realize that God is the originator, orchestrator, and the perfecter of all things. He had a grand plan right from the beginning, and He hasn't changed His mind. So why should you as a child of God wander without direction, finding it difficult to connect with His purpose for your life in terms of finding your God-ordained partner? You need to repent from writing your own love story and let God wow you with a well-crafted manuscript of your heavenly-orchestrated love story. It will be beyond anything Hollywood can comprehend or reproduce because it will be so out of this world.

Now that you've come to this realization that God is the one who does the finding after preparing the man and woman, you must identify the role you play and how to go about receiving from God. The analogy I gave in the preface describes God as a stage-setter, a scriptwriter who has the script in His hands and knows exactly how He wants this movie to play out. He places every actor where they ought to be to bring the story to life. Dear brother or sister, your love story has been pre-written by God; just let Him position you where you need to be to make the story complete. He is only waiting for you to release yourself to Him and trust that He has this all set up perfectly.

Common Mistakes Singles Make

Many single people find themselves making the following mistakes that keeps them going in circles of failed relationships, heartbreaks, and not finding a connection to the right person:

Using unrealistic checklists.

It's great to have a checklist, but how realistic is your checklist? Checklists should have the major things you cannot compromise on. For example, the number one thing I've always had on my mental checklist when I was single was a God-fearing man, which meant he had to be a Christian, but not just a Christian. He had to be a practicing and dedicated one. I was not going to compromise on faith no matter what. There were other things on my list as well, such as education level, race, height, and physical appearance. You have to determine what you are never going to compromise on and determine what you can be more open about, such as height, looks, culture, and so forth.

> While checklists are great for identifying potential partners, they can also limit you from finding the right person.

While checklists are great for identifying potential partners, they can also limit you from finding the right person. For example, if you are a man who is determined to find a six-foot-tall woman, you could miss out on God's plan simply because God brought to you a woman who was 5'8". If you dated anyone before or have been in a relationship with anyone before, I would like to encourage you to do this little exercise of reflection: think about people you're usually attracted to or people you've dated in the past. Have they all met the criteria on your checklist? Why didn't that relationship work?

If you have a type and have always been able to date your "type," but things never worked out, you just might need to review your list to highlight what's important or simply start a new one. Maybe what you think you want isn't what is good for you or isn't what God wants for you. You must come to that realization and make changes as soon as possible.

Not involving God.
One of the biggest mistakes anyone can ever make is to not involve God in the things they do. This has been explicitly explained in chapter two of this book. When you make the mistake of excluding God from the equation, you are heading directly for a dead end. Don't be surprised when you crash. Nevertheless, there is good news for you if you haven't gone too far. If you realize you've not always involved God in your dating world, you can start now, and you will be amazed at the difference this makes. The most gracious thing about our God is that He gives us the grace to make changes that allows Him to prove himself as the Almighty in our lives.

The costliest mistake Christians make is not realizing the power of the God we have until we are in trouble. If you've always run back to God after a breakup, asking why you, is it possible that you've been doing it your way which hasn't yielded much for you? I advise you to make it a typical practice to always involve God in everything you do, starting with the thought of being ready to date. From there, involve God in every step of the dating process. If it is His will, He will direct your path, and everything will work together for good for those who love and trust Him.

I would like to point out that there are people who believe they *have* involved God in their decision-making process for who to date and marry. But after marriage, those relationships don't work. What do we then say in such cases? As Christians, we can only try our best in terms of making decisions and seeking the will of God, and if sometimes things don't turn out the way we expect, we still learn valuable lessons for the future. You can learn more about yourself, the other person, the dynamics of relationships, life, and God.

Assuming everyone in church is datable.

As a young Christian, you ought to desire to be with a fellow Christian so you can continue to grow and be made perfect in the love of Christ. However, with this desire, you should be careful not to be deceived because the devil's agents can be sent to infiltrate the church disguised as Christians. Yes, not every so-called Christian is a true Christian. There are many church-going Christians actively involved in ministries and serving faithfully, but their conduct outside the church does not reflect being a Christian.

The Bible warns in 1 John 4:1 that we are not to believe every spirit but to test the spirits to see whether they are from God. While there are no perfect people on earth and certainly not in the church, we ought to be mindful not to equate church participation or attendance with having a relationship with God. There are some people who specifically go to church to find potential dates. This is a good idea, but the problem then lies in not knowing their true intentions about God. While there are genuine people, there are also deceptive people in church. May the Holy Spirit guide you in all truth to be able to discern well.

Not knowing your role.

This goes in line of what was explained earlier in this chapter about the role of God, the role of man, and the role of the woman. These days, I have witnessed men saying that women should be doing the finding. This is because a lot of ladies don't want to wait. They claim they are being bold, being non-traditional, being modern, and seeing what they want and then going for it, but this makes it too easy for some men to take advantage of a woman they don't really want. This can also make it difficult for a man to identify who is really good for them or who God is positioning before them.

Being desperate.

This mistake happens when you can't wait on God, and you decide to write your own love story. The point of desperation is letting other factors other than God be your reason for looking to date. The first sign of desperation is when you have a sense of urgency to date or to get someone to commit to you. The urgency is what you need to pay attention to.

Don't let age, people, your unrealistic expectations, timelines, and other people push you to a point of desperation. "Be still and know that I am God" (Psalm 46:10). That Bible verse can help you avoid desperation. When you catch yourself being desperate, pray about it, slow down, and let God lead you in the right path. The danger in being desperate is that you will assume everything is perfect, you will not see a need to assess if the person you're dating is right for you, you become vulnerable, and in some cases, your desperation scares a potential partner away. Yes, you can scare potential partners away. When you hear a date saying, "You're coming on too strong," you need to pay attention and make changes as soon as possible. Slow down! Get your mind right, don't get too excited, be patient with the process, and remember that you are only just getting to know this person; they may or may not be the right one for you.

Being undiscerning.

Being undiscerning means to lack judgment or insight. This can be tied to many things, but one is desperation that you've just read about. Desperation affects your ability to discern right. The spirit of discernment is totally dependent on both God and you aligning well. It requires spiritual, physical, and mental alertness. To determine the right path, you must be completely mindful and in a state of calmness to be able to carefully observe, gather useful information, think critically, pray diligently, check, reassess, and get confirmation from God. These are necessary steps to take to be able to decide if a person is right for you or not.

How to Avoid These Mistakes

What do you do in this searching and waiting phase to avoid the mistakes highlighted above? I encourage you to consider doing the following:

Give yourself to God in prayers…be connected to God. Commit your ways to the lord, trust also in Him and He shall bring it to pass (Psalm 37:5).

Seek God's guidance. This can be done by praying and letting God direct you. You can also seek spiritual support from your trusted prayer partner and pastor.

Make yourself available and be open-minded (Ruth 2:1-13).

Stay productive. As discussed earlier, be like Adam and Ruth who were productive and eventually were connected to their God-given partner.

Be diligent in everything you do. You never know who is watching. You may become linked to your ideal partner by someone who has always known you. Be mindful of your way of life, your actions, and the way you relate to people, and continue to invest in yourself. Just work toward being the best version of yourself and the right person will be connected to you at the right time. The right time is something you can't know, can't plan for, and can't be too prepared for. However, when you are diligent in

41

all you do, you will fit right into the picture when the right time comes.

Watch and wait. Psalm 37:7a says, "Rest in the Lord and wait patiently for him." Be alert and on the lookout. Watching and waiting in this context means being expectant. When you are expecting something, you need to prepare for it, and you need to create a space for it. You need to be ready for it and you need to have the mental capacity for it. In this case, as a spiritually inclined Christian, you need to be watchful both spiritually and physically. It also means being openminded, because in this critical stage, you don't want to miss this blessing of a God-given partner coming your way.

Watching also means you believe God will do something for you, and while you are expecting it, be encouraged to patiently wait for it. Waiting requires a deep level of trust that He will fulfill His promise. The

> When you are expecting something, you need to prepare for it!

encouragement for you during this time of waiting is in the Philippians 4:6, which states, "Do not be anxious for anything in every situation, with prayers and thanksgiving, make your requests known to the Lord." The temptation to become anxious is great, especially when you have your own timeline, and it seems like it's approaching or has passed. Indeed, perhaps both family and friends are starting to put pressure on you. Please be encouraged and remember to give thanks, be joyful, and trust in God. He is never late. Remember His words, "For the vision is for an appointed time, though it tarries, wait for it, it will surely come" (Habakkuk 2:3).

While you are watching and waiting, your friends might be getting around you, increasing the pressure even more. Just be joyful and expectant because something great is coming your way, and God is planning to blow your mind. He will never forsake you. If you've been waiting for a long time and you've given up hope because, in your eyes, your time has passed, then remember that such is your conclusion, not God's verdict over your life. I encourage you to trust God more and receive hope in His Word as stated in Jeremiah 29:11: "He knows the plans he has for you, the thought of good and not of evil, to prosper you and bring you to an expected end." God's plan is not for you to be depressed while waiting. It's not for you to give up on Him, and it's not for you to resent others who seem to be getting it right. There is absolutely nothing wrong with you. The fact that you are still single is not an indication of a deficiency.

Please be happy in your single and waiting phase. This should be the best time of your life where you build an intimate relationship with God to the fullness of His blessings. Spend time enjoying the presence of God and doing the things you love. Do you know how much of a blessing the gift of time is? Make the best out of your single days. I wish I had taken more time to travel in my single days, to be clearer on my life goals, and to pursue what I found more desirable for me. If you want to travel, please do. If you want to write a book, go ahead and do it. If you want to move to a new city, start a business, learn something new, or socialize or network more, then go for it!

God will beautify your life and make you whole as a single person. There is something astonishing about being whole, that is, to be complete in God, independent by yourself but dependent on Him alone. Do not let your life and happiness be dependent on another human being. This is what you must realize before you go into a relationship, and when you find yourself in a relationship or marriage, there is no guarantee that your partner will make you happy all the time. You are responsible for your own happiness, with God being your source of joy and fulfillment. Let God complete you and prepare your mind and heart for a person who will complement you.

Chapter Three Questions

1. Do you have a checklist of what you are looking for in a potential partner?

2. Is your checklist realistic?

3. Are you prepared for what you are looking for?

4. What changes do you need to make in your searching and waiting phase? (For example, have you been attracting the wrong set of people or are you looking in the wrong place for the wrong reasons?)

5. What do you need to do as you prepare to connect with your God-given partner?

CHAPTER FOUR
Decision Making Phase: Identification & Selection of a Potential Partner

After starting with God, preparing yourself, and waiting, you should ask yourself what's next and how do you identify someone you can date? What kind of person should you be searching and waiting for? This chapter will focus on the process of identifying and selecting a potential partner.

I can tell you confidently that the Spirit of God is able to guide you in all truth and will not mislead you. In the watching and waiting phase, potential partners came your way. You might have noticed some and others you paid no mind, depending on how well they fit

> *The first item on your list should be what you cannot compromise on—a must have on your list.*

your mental checklist. Now is the time to thoroughly sift through your options, which can be done by communicating or relating with the people you meet. You want to make sure you are having meaningful and tactful conversations to get to know more about a person.

Let's talk about your options. Can you date several people at the same time? If you go by the definition of dating provided in chapter one, then yes, you can date or talk to more than one person without making commitments to any of them. This is a "no strings attached" approach. At this stage, you are simply meeting people and looking to see which of them has the potential to be your God-given partner. This is why you need to date plainly and simply. Date with your head and not your heart.

Dating with your head means you guard your heart and won't easily fall in out-of-control love without knowing the person. Dating with your heart is when you fall in love easily without the ability to think logically. A heart-led person only depends on feelings despite any wrong signs. These types of people believe that "the heart wants what it wants." Remember the analogy of an interview given in chapter one? This is a stage where you put on the mindset of an interviewer or maybe an investigator who needs to make sure an applicant fits their requirements. An interviewer doesn't just offer a job to every single applicant that indicates interest in a job. They tend to take their time in the interview if given the chance.

In the case of a single person, you don't have to set a time limit that hinders your ability to assess. Be open to options, especially when you are not sure about a person. Don't fall prey to the worldly philosophy that states you should make a commitment to someone simply because you had several dates with them. This doesn't have to be your standard. This is your life and your decision to make. Set your own standards. You can take your time to be friends with potential dates. Get to know them first. Don't feel pressured to make a commitment of going into a relationship if you don't feel the need to.

I will use myself as an example here. While I was very guarded about opening up my heart to just anybody, I also did not give myself enough time to be single and enjoy my singleness. I turned down some guys without giving enough chance to date them because I thought I knew what I wanted and chose to date those I thought were a good fit. I ended up committing to a relationship with the ones I felt more connected to and then went on in a relationship for at least two to three years with them.

Approaching and Connecting

Guy meets girl.

Now on to the stage of playing your role. For a guy, you've met a girl through some means. You can meet people randomly in unexpected places or recurrently at locations where you both typically go, such as gym, work, class, and so on. You can meet people through friends, family, social media, and through other means.

Let's take some time on the topic of where to *find* a potential date. There is no limit to where you can find someone to date in this day and age, especially with the many online opportunities. Sliding into DMs on Instagram and Facebook messaging, Snap Chat connections, and other social media sources make it easier for people to connect these days. And these should not be ruled out as mediums of meeting people, especially in the current tech age, but you should apply the same rules you use to meet someone in person. Be careful to prayerfully discern who is good for you.

Using myself as an example, my husband found me on one of the social media platforms through mutual friends. This was at a time in my life when I was praying for my God-given partner in total surrender to God. I wouldn't have thought that the answer to my prayer would come through a social media avenue of connection. I hereby encourage you to be open-minded when you pray to God so that you can carefully discern when He answers your prayers. I know of several people who have met their spouses online and things worked out just fine. But there are also some that didn't work out. So, regardless of how you meet a person, the point is that you do meet and begin to get to know each other.

> I hereby encourage you to be open-minded when you pray to God so that you can carefully discern when He answers your prayers.

So, as a guy, you need to make a move to approach that girl like a gentleman, genuinely wanting to get to know her. Gentlemanly behavior is when you approach a lady softly, sweetly, smoothly, and genuinely. This requires a relaxed and friendly body language without being creepy or aggressive. Ladies like when guys notice them, approach them with respect, and engage them in a conversation that makes the woman feel comfortable, heard, and respected. Creepy is when you meet a woman and you completely undress her with your eyes, make quirky comments about her body, don't respect personal space, or you come off too strong. She can smell that mess from a far distance. A lady who knows her worth will not condone it. As a Christian brother, you should not be caught in that creepy web; that's not a characteristic of a true Christian. It will only make a Christian lady rule you out.

For a lady who is single and ready to mingle, it is a time of positioning yourself in a way that a man will find you approachable. If you are meeting in person, your appearance, body language, and the people you hang out with matters a lot. It's not always easy for some guys to just approach a lady they do not know, because they don't know how she will react. If you are always frowning or somewhat stand-offish, you might affect your approachability, preventing some guys from introducing themselves to you. So, be aware of the way you carry yourself and what message you are sending to people.

A guy once told me of a particular girl he liked, but every time he saw her, she was always with her mean-looking sister, and he was afraid the sister would stop him if he tried to approach her. In this situation, it wasn't her, but the person she hung out with who was hindering access to her. I know of guys and girls with bad attitudes, who were just completely arrogant and rude, feeling like they were too good for certain types of people. But they can drive away their "type" with that kind of attitude. Girls, you never know what will attract a man to you; it could be your smile, the way you carry yourself, the way you relate with others, the way you speak, or how friendly you are and many other things you do.

If we follow the story of Adam and Eve, the role of the guy is to rest in the Lord and let God bring the woman to his attention. Likewise, the role of the lady is to be yielding, willing, and open to receive when he finds you.

The main message here for both guys and ladies is for you to ensure you are doing good, being pleasant, being cheerful, being productive, and being the best version of yourself (Psalm 37:3). The parable of the ten virgins comes to mind here. Five virgins were prepared with extra oil for their lamp. I can imagine that they also had their outfits ready along with everything else they needed for the bridegroom to find them worthy. In the same way, you must be prepared at all times to receive the bridegroom (Matthew 25:1-13).

Since this book is targeted to single Christians, the number one thing to look for in a potential partner is to make sure he or she is a born-again Christian. I should pause here and ask you: are you a born-again Christian? A born-again Christian is a practicing Christian who has given his or her life to Christ and has died to sin to take on a new life in Christ, making a conscious effort to walk daily in His ways, developing a relationship with Him, and having the fear of God. It is important for you to be a born-again Christian to be able to identify "the one."

I explained this difference so you can be wise enough to look beyond a church-going Christian. You need to know how close they are to God and assess whether their way of life matches what they profess. Yes, people can tell you anything to worm their way into your heart, but you, as a child of God, must see to it that you are not deceived by sweet words. You've got some work to do. Yes, you've got to find answers to these questions, and it will take time and some strategies by communicating, investigating, and confirming.

And it is those three things that should take place in the dating phase. In this phase, when you meet someone, you take time to get to know them *without making a commitment.* I emphasized "without making a commitment" because at this phase you are only trying to find out if this person is worthy of making a commitment to. Unfortunately, this is where many people get too

51

excited and skip this important aspect that can possibly help them identify and eliminate incompatible dates. Dating is that essential platonic phase that you must not take lightly and must approach intentionally and strategically.

One of the challenges and complicated aspects of the dating phase is the popular concept of "love at first sight." I used to believe in this, but I later discovered that it is not love at first sight. It is rather attraction at first sight, which is a normal occurrence. You are always attracted to something you see and like. It's nearly the same for material things, clothes, cars, food, and so on. I don't say this to spoil your belief but to help you see potential traps and misleading situations. I must admit that there are many people who ended up marrying someone they were attracted to at first sight, but there are

> I used to believe in this, but I later discovered that it is not love at first sight. It is rather attraction at first sight, which is a normal occurrence.

some who found each other incompatible, so other factors definitely come into play.

This is why I encourage you to approach this carefully. Like I mentioned earlier, it's human and completely normal to be initially attracted to someone who fits your "type." If you meet a beautiful girl or a handsome man, it's perfectly okay and normal for you to be enamored by their attractiveness. Nevertheless, you must control yourself not to be over-smitten and consumed only by what you see. This is why Proverbs 31:30 says that "Charm is deceptive, and beauty is fleeting." Therefore, dear brother or sister, the feeling you have at first sight is not quite love; it is mere attraction. It can, however, be a good sign because there is already something you like about that person, but you just have to look a little deeper.

There is also a possibility that you didn't quite become attracted to someone at first sight, but that does not mean they aren't good for you. Did you catch that? I have seen people who weren't initially attracted to their husbands and wives but ended up marrying each other after getting to know one another. I have also seen people who wrote off some potential partners they didn't find attractive and ended up not liking the one they found attractive. You should keep an open mind and get to know a person before disqualifying them.

An unrelenting, extremely detailed checklist can be your number one barrier to finding your God-given partner. This brings us to the topic of "your type."

Let's take some time to delve into the topic of "type." This word is commonly used to describe a certain kind of person you would typically date while ruling out others. For example, a guy might decide that his type of girl should be independent, well educated (to be more specific, a girl with a graduate degree), at least 5'8" tall, high maintenance, light skinned, of a certain race, and outgoing. This guy's description rules out a lot of other people. So, if he meets a girl who is 5'7" tall with a graduate degree and meets all his other requirements, he might rule her out because she does not meet his minimum height standard. As you process this, I encourage you to reflect on your life and what your "type" is.

> What is your *type* of guy or lady?

➢ How has it been since you've been dating your type?

➢ How many of your type have you dated and why didn't it work out with them?

➢ Have you been limiting yourself by the type of person you've chosen to align yourself with?

➢ Would you be open to loosening up on your type to allow God to lead you to make the best choice with more than you can imagine?

The beautiful thing about not boxing God in is that you allow Him to make a masterpiece that will knock you off your feet. Yes, He will do it!

Therefore, rather than being limited by a list, keep the following things in mind:

Determine what is most important to you in a potential partner. The first item on your list should be what you cannot compromise on—a must have on your list. I would suggest as a Christian that you prioritize all things that involve God. When I was single, my number one thing was finding a God-fearing man. While you can't quite know who is a God-fearing person immediately, you should start off with making sure the person is at least a Christian. As a Christian, if God is utmost in your heart and if you started your journey with God, it is paramount for you to identify God in the person you want to be with. I have come to the realization that the level in which people prioritize God in relationships reflects their relationship with God.

Determine other things you can't absolutely tolerate in a potential partner

Be flexible in terms of what is important to look for in a potential partner and don't be too rigid on your "type" or list.

Make sure he or she is a born-again Christian. There are biblical guidelines to buttress this point in 2 Corinthians 6:14, which states, "Do not be unequally yoked together with unbelievers. For what fellowship has righteousness with lawlessness? And what communion has light with darkness?"

To get a full understanding of this verse, there is need for an explanation of the keywords "unequally yoked." The online Cambridge Dictionary describes being yoked as "a wooden bar fastened over the necks of two animals, especially cattle, so that they are fastened together and to a connected vehicle or load."[5] The "unequal" part is very straightforward. It means not equal. This description makes it clear that when two people, in the context of the Bible verse, are unequally yoked, they can't be well aligned. Their journey becomes turbulent and exhausting as one person will bear the burden more than the other.

The following highlighted points summarize the points made in this chapter and should serve as a guideline for determining and selecting your potential partner (someone you decide to date).

Notice the word *potential* because this doesn't mean they are the one yet.

> ➤ **Pray and carefully discern** with wisdom (shine your eyes). Beware of time wasters! There will always be several options out there, but a God-given option is very

---

[5] "Yoked." *Cambridge Dictionary,* Cambridge Advanced Learner Dictionary and Thesaurus. https://dictionary.cambridge.org/us/dictionary/english/yokedAccessed 15 Jan. 2022.

unique and rare. "Beloved, do not believe every spirit, but test the spirits, whether they are of God; because many false prophets have gone out into the world" (1 John 4:1). Another scripture warns in Romans 16:17-18, "I urge you, brothers, and sisters, to watch out for those who cause divisions and put obstacles in your way that are contrary to the teaching you have learned. Keep away from them. For such people are not serving our Lord Christ, but their own appetites. By smooth talk and flattery they deceive the minds of naive people."

➤ **Assess** based on your values and personal standards.

➤ **Find their convictions** by asking them specific questions, doing research, and doing soul searching.

➤ **Communicate** and find out each other's goals for life, relationship, and more. Are they dating for fun or to marry?

➤ **Determine whether to proceed or not.**

➤ **Agree on your relationship.** State what this stage means for you.

➤ **Discuss boundaries** based on your values (example: no sex, going public, and so on).

Chapter Four Questions

1. Have you ever prayed and asked God to lead you in identifying your potential partner? If so, have you yielded to Him or did you move ahead based on your desires alone?

2. Are you willing to let God lead you in this process?

3. Do you need to revisit your "type" specifications or requirements? If so, write them out.

4. What have you learned about yourself based on the content of this chapter?

5. What would you start doing differently to identify and select a potential partner?

CHAPTER FIVE
Dating Phase: Compatibility Check

What do you do after you've made the decision to date one another? In this stage, you are building a friendship. I hope you still remember the definition of dating I gave in chapter one. In summary, dating is a stage in which two people get to know each other to determine if they are compatible enough to have a meaningful and committed relationship. This is a critical stage that you don't want to miss. You want to really get to know the person, what they like and dislike, what their hobbies are, how they interact with people, how they react to situations, and many other things. In this stage, you are scratching the surface of their personality and character layer by layer. If you go too deep too

This is not the stage to relax and feel like you've got it. The work has just begun.

fast, you will doubtlessly miss very important things you need to know. It is important to be open to one another but also be careful what information you divulge, bearing in mind that you haven't made any serious commitments to each other. You've only identified this person as a strong potential of being the one, but you still need to tread carefully and be discerning.

This newest stage is not the stage to relax and feel like you've got it. No, the work has just begun. All you did before this stage was to prepare for this stage, which is only meant to prepare you for the next stage. This is a step-by-step guide. Proceed into this stage with your five senses alert, like an investigator gathering all the necessary information before making a reasonable and informed decision. My dear brother and sister, I earnestly encourage you to proceed into this stage by guarding your heart from falling in love too quickly. Avoid distractions while focusing on the right things. I can't emphasize this enough, but at this stage, you are only building a platonic friendship that could possibly evolve into a committed relationship with the purpose of getting married.

In truth, dating someone in this stage means you will naturally start developing feelings for this person. After all, they made it this far by meeting many of your criteria as a potential partner, but please don't start planning a wedding in your head yet. Just pull the brakes and have several conversations with yourself to stay focused every step of the way. You are still getting to know each other.

This falling in love stage is what a lot of people use as the major sign to determine that this person is the one, but beware! As wonderful as such emotions might feel, it is only a feeling that will pass after a while. Feelings can be very misleading sometimes, and I would like to address the common philosophy of "following your heart." As a Christian, you ought to be careful not to make this concept an anchor for your life but to follow the biblical text: "However, when He, the Spirit of truth, has come, He will guide you into all truth; for He will not speak on His own authority, but whatever He hears He will speak; and He will tell you things to come" (John 16:13). This means that you should follow the Holy Spirit's lead and ensure that your heart is filled with the Spirit. A Spirit-filled heart should not be carnally focused and feeling-based. It is led by the truth of the Word of God.

This phase is very important in your dating journey. Whether you end up getting married or not, you want to make sure you leave a good and long-lasting impression on each other. With this, if you don't end up together, you can still appreciate your friendship. And if you do end up getting married, you will treasure this phase forever, knowing it is here that you watched each other work through differences. So, when, in marriage, you have a fight, you will remember how you started, the friendship that took time to build, and what you love about each other. Yes, you are building a strong foundation of love at this stage, and you want to make sure you build it correctly and firmly.

Like I mentioned earlier, it is only natural for you to have feelings for the person you date. However, it is not yet time to start saying, "I love you," or "I think I'm in love with you." Slow down! Remember that: slow down! At this point, it's okay to say, "I like you," and find other ways to make it known. For example, you can say, "I enjoy talking to you," or "I appreciate the time we spend together," or "you make me laugh." You can show some affection but be very plain, sweet, and focused. The mission again is to get to know each other and arrive at a conclusion on if you want to proceed to the next stage with them and make a commitment to each other in courtship. I'll teach all about courtship in subsequent chapters.

As you proceed through this stage, please be sure to keep your checklist handy. It might not be a physical checklist, but you probably have certain things in mind. The more you get to know a person the more you confirm their true character and how much they match your checklist. If you would like to be with a God-fearing person, this is the stage where you get to know the person more and see how God-fearing they truly are. While there are tons of things you should be checking for, a few are enumerated below.

Level of Maturity

Indicators of maturity can be found in how a person thinks, how they assess and respond to situations, how they communicate, and if they are emotionally intelligent. When I was dating, I assessed a man's level of maturity by how logical, reasonable, considerate, attentive, engaged, relatable, respectful, and compassionate they are...among other things.

> The more you get to know a person the more you confirm their true character and how much they match your checklist.

That might seem like a lot, but there is more to it. It all hinges around your ability to relate to a person. I have always been a big communicator, and I leave no stone unturned in the beginning. I must admit that I'm a hopeless romantic who guards my heart carefully before giving it away. A person like me who loves wholeheartedly doesn't play around when considering someone to date. I approach dating with all my antennas well-tuned and alert. I ask questions, fact check statements, and call out whatever doesn't sound right. I was always very particular about a person's character.

You will need to attain some level of maturity to be able to judge someone else's level of maturity. This isn't to say I always got it right. I have also made dating mistakes, but God has been faithful to reorder my steps to align with His will. Not everyone is what they present themselves to be, and it takes God's revelation to know the truth. The message here is for you to make sure you at least possess some qualities or attributes you are looking for in someone else, because a person with the right intention will also be looking for key attributes in you.

Spiritual Life

So, you have identified that this potential partner has a relationship with the Lord in the previous stage, but now is the time for you to know more about their spiritual life. Where are they strong or weak? How can you both help each other to grow spiritually?

A major mistake any young Christian will make is to assume that spirituality is not important in a relationship. The truth is that the institution of marriage itself is orchestrated spiritually. Take a look at the way the need for a companion emanated from a deep relationship Adam had with God. After God had become so close to Adam, He realized that Adam needed another human to walk life's journey with him, to stay with him in the garden, and to support him so they can both fulfill God's purpose together. It should be the same for you and your potential partner. Each of you should've been building your spiritual lives before meeting each other. It is now time for you to align spiritually.

Know Each Other's Goals and Align Them

You've probably heard the common saying that "the person you marry can either make or break you." That simply means the person you marry and how well you both believe in each other's life goals will determine how you will support one another toward achieving it.

Your goals don't have to be exactly the same, but you want to make sure you are genuinely interested in supporting them toward achieving their life's goals, whether it's your area of interest or not. For example, if a man's goal is to start an ecommerce business and the wife's goal is to start a non-profit business, aligning your goals means setting timelines together to when you would like to achieve each. This gives you an idea of the priorities you have ahead of you if you decide to proceed into marriage.

Another example is of two people in undergrad studies and hoping to establish a serious relationship. They too need to discuss how they want to align their goals. In this case, one person has a goal of going to medical school after undergrad work and the other plans to start working immediately with a plan to start a master's degree two years later. They need to discuss how to accommodate each other's goals so they can support each other and make plans how to manage their relationship through it all.

This process helps couples to understand each other better, know each other's goals, and determine whether they can accommodate those goals. I know of a relationship that was discontinued as a result of one of the two being unwilling to accommodate the other person's goal of furthering their education. If your goal is not well received, acknowledged, and supported by your date, you should carefully discern if that is a positive relationship for you.

Compatibility Check

One of the major reasons for dating is to check how compatible you are with a person. You surely have heard of many divorces due to irreconcilable differences and you probably have wondered why that's the case. While unforeseen circumstances happen in life, it is important to take the time in the beginning to do a compatibility check. This is to see how well you both get along, what can be a deal breaker, how different you are, and what you cannot overlook about each other.

I hate to break it to you, but marriage is an eye opener, a revealer. In marriage, you see everything about your partner, the good and the bad, but if you do this dating stage right, you won't be too shocked after marriage and want to run away. At this dating stage, you want to make sure you and your partner get along and understand each other.

Some people tend to confuse being compatible with being alike when it doesn't necessarily mean that. Being compatible, according to the Oxford Dictionary, literally means "two things being able to exist or occur together without conflict."[6] As you check for compatibility, you want to look at physical, emotional, spiritual, and intellectual compatibility. In each of these categories, you should ask yourself specific questions.

Physical Compatibility

There is a common saying that beauty is in the eyes of the beholder. It is important to establish physical compatibility by making sure you are physically attracted to your boyfriend or girlfriend. So, you need to ask yourself, do I love what I see? Do I like this person's physique (look, walk, complexion, height, and so on)?

---

[6] "Compatible." Hornby, Albert Sydney. Oxford Advanced Learner's Dictionary of Current English / [by] A.S. Hornby ; Editor Jonathan Crowther. Oxford, England :Oxford University Press, 1995, https://www.oxfordlearnersdictionaries.com/us/definition/english/compatible. Accessed 25 January 2022.

Emotional Compatibility

Emotional compatibility can be identified by relating with this person over time and getting to know if you appeal to each other emotionally. Do you feel a connection from relating with one another? Are you both able to manage your emotions well enough to have a healthy and meaningful relationship?

Intellectual Compatibility

This can be a common sense or IQ check where you identify if you are comfortable with your boyfriend or girlfriend's level of intelligence. You would at least expect that this person has common sense and can think logically and have meaningful conversations to get things done in life. There are people who have a strong preference for people who have a high IQ. It is therefore in your hands to determine what level of IQ will work well for you.

Ask, can this person have meaningful ideas that support my vision and positively influence our relationship? Do we respect and accept each other's level of intelligence? There are people who don't consider this aspect while dating but end up becoming frustrated later in life. You need to determine if you are comfortable with your potential partner's level of intelligence.

Spiritual Compatibility

This is another important one that assesses how well each individual's spiritual life complements one another. Do each person's level of spirituality and spiritual values align to help each other and glorify God? Your spiritual lives should always have God at the center without confusion or division as is stated in 1 Corinthians 10:25.

I once met a guy who was interested in dating me. We talked for some time, but the more I got to know him as a person the more evidence I found to determine that he wasn't the right one for me. His way of life and the way he communicated was somewhat controversial…despite seeming like a devoted Christian who was in a leadership role in his church. His actions and words did not reflect strong level of maturity, and that was a major disconnect for me. I questioned his level of maturity, I questioned his spirituality as a Christian whom other people were looking up to, and finally, he was quite manipulative in getting attention, exhibiting narcissistic traits. I called out his unacceptable behaviors, was politely honest with him about my observation, and told him I wasn't interested in being with him. If he was already stressing me out and pressuring me to feed his narcissism when I hadn't made any commitment to date him, then I couldn't imagine what being with him would actually be like. Frankly, I wasn't interested in finding out.

It is important to check for compatibility while dating as a precautionary measure to determine if the attributes you notice in a person are acceptable to you.

It is important to check for compatibility while dating as a precautionary measure to determine if the attributes you notice in a person are acceptable to you. The Austin Institute for the Study of

Family and Culture,[7] using data from 4,000 divorced adults, identified the top reasons for divorce as the following:

1. Spouse unresponsive to needs

2. Incompatibility

3. Spouse immaturity

4. Emotional abuse

5. Financial problems

This information buttresses the need to check for compatibility, maturity and the other attributes highlighted here.

Finally, the purpose of checking compatibility is to determine if you can like each other well enough while respecting your differences. More questions you can consider asking to determine compatibility are as follows:

➢ What do I like about this person?

➢ How much do they match my checklist?

➢ How compatible are we?

➢ What don't I like about this person and is it a deal breaker?

---

[7] The Austin Institute for the Study of Family and Culture, "Relationships in America Survey," 2014. Retrieved Aug 11, 2022, from www.thearda.com/data-archive?fid=FS14.

Chapter Five Questions

1. What are your major takeaways from this chapter?

2. If you've been in a relationship before, what type of relationship patterns or habits have you formed?

3. What is your plan for conducting a compatibility and maturity check?

4. Are you going to be honest with yourself and do a maturity check on yourself in preparation for your potential partner?

5. What would you start doing differently?

CHAPTER SIX
Courtship Phase: Let's Make It Official

Dear reader, please bear in mind that the transition from one stage to another in this relationship guide (chapter to chapter) is an opportunity to reflect, assess, and apply to your life. This book is written with the expectation that you are intentionally applying these principles in your life.

So, you have come this far in your journey to find your God-given partner. But regardless of how you move from stage to stage, you will still have questions, hoping to God that you are making the right decision. This is a completely normal feeling, but it is important to channel that feeling into prayers, asking for the Holy Spirit's guidance. Always keep in mind the scripture in John 16:13

> *It's not a trial-and-error union. It's a relationship you've prayed about, and you've seen a sign from God and believe you are being led by the Holy Spirit to proceed.*

which speaks of how the Holy Spirit will guide you in all truth. Your spiritual alertness is what helps you receive the guidance needed from the Holy Spirit.

The more time you spend getting to know each other, the more you would naturally fall in love with one another. However, remember that you are yet to make a full commitment to one another. You've built a meaningful friendship to this point, are interested in one another, enjoy spending time together, and are excited about being in each other's lives. Indeed, you feel butterflies anytime you think about, see, talk to, and hear about each other. This is a great feeling to have and it's important for your relationship. It shows how emotionally connected you've become and how your relationship is evolving from platonic to something that can be more substantial.

Nevertheless, we cannot be oblivious to the possibility that this might not happen for some people. It is possible to spend time getting to know someone and then realize that you don't belong together. In such cases, you should not proceed any further if you don't see a future together. However, if you've determined after getting to know each other that you want to proceed to the next stage and would like to be more committed to one another, then you can make it "official."

If you've gone through the compatibility check stage and determined you are compatible with one another, have mutual feelings of love, have an understanding of one another's goals in life, and are willing to walk together in this journey called life, you should discuss making it "official." This change will not be in the context of marriage but move you both into courtship. You would, at this stage, agree that you are compatible, you are in love, you have prayed and confirmed that you want to be together, and you believe you get along well enough to be in a relationship called courtship.

What Is Courtship?

As mentioned in the preceding chapters, courtship is a period during which a couple develops a romantic relationship with the intention of marriage. It's not a trial-and-error union; it's a relationship you've prayed about, you've seen a sign from God, and you believe you are being led by the Holy Spirit to proceed.

Keep in mind that this does not mean you are married yet. Don't get too carried away with the thought that marriage is in view. You still need to continue to pray and invest in yourselves individually and as a couple. Let God lead you and be careful not to live like a married couple yet.

I hate to break it to you, but simply because you made it this far does not mean this person is "the one" and it doesn't guarantee marriage. However, if you've both spiritually sought the face of the Lord and have received mutual confirmation from above, you do need to start preparing your minds toward marriage. Therefore, you must tread carefully so you won't fall so deep that you are unable to pull yourself out if needed.

This stage is similar to the previous stage except now you are getting to know yourselves on a deeper level with a commitment to determine if you want the official lifelong commitment. In most cases, for Christians who have learned how to hear from God and are ready for marriage, you both probably know you want to marry each other and have an idea when you want to finalize it. This was the case for my husband and me. When we agreed to make a commitment to court, we knew we were going to get married. Our hope and plan were toward marriage. Prior to meeting my husband,

I had also been in a relationship/courtship for at least three years that didn't end in marriage.

Courtship is a time to prepare yourselves toward aligning your personal goals, life purpose, and marital goals together. I can also describe this stage as a formation process or marriage-prep stage. In this stage, you are beginning to cleave to one another. Let's review what happened when Adam first sighted Eve in the Garden of Eden in Genesis 2:23. He saw her, named her, embraced her, and called her his. If you are able to identify yourselves as God's choice for one another, congratulations! It is time to get serious about the kind of marriage you've been praying for, how you both want to prepare for or approach marriage and assess each other's level of maturity and readiness for marriage.

> *Courtship is a time to prepare yourselves toward aligning your personal goals, life purpose, and marital goals together.*

Well, the truth is, no one is ever fully ready for marriage because we learn and grow as we journey on in life. However, the ability to prepare your mind for marriage can be an added advantage when entering marriage.

The next step is to start walking together, identifying your strengths and weaknesses, and determining how you want to grow together while complementing one another. The mistake many couples make is establishing their relationship on love alone. While love is important in every relationship, there are many factors that come into play in building upon that love. The work you put into the love you have is what sustains a relationship. This is why you hear people say, "Love is not enough," while some people would argue, "Love is all you need." Now let's take a deep dive into the world of love to get a better understanding of what this lovely word really means that's been so concerningly abused and misused.

What Is Love?

The real gospel truth is that "love" in the Bible context is all you need. Earlier in chapter one, there was a brief mention of love as stated in 1 John 4:8, which says, "For he who does not love does not know God, God is Love." This Bible verse helps to put love in the proper context. "God is love," which serves as the noun aspect of love. God embodies love and this is one of the reasons why you must start with God.

Additionally, the Bible also speaks of love in many more instances but particularly in 1 Corinthians 13:4-8, where it describes love as the greatest of gifts, proffering several adjectives for love and laying out what love is and is not. This Bible passage states: "Love suffers long *and* is kind; love does not envy; love does not parade itself, is not puffed up; does not behave rudely, does not seek its own, is not provoked, thinks no evil; does not rejoice in iniquity, but rejoices in the truth; bears all things, believes all things, hopes all things, endures all things. Love never fails."

Contrary to popular opinion, love is not just a feeling. Though it is abstract, it is not passive as its descriptions imply. Love is an action word. The product of your acts and expressions of love then produces a pleasant feeling that makes people feel loved. Love is beautiful and pure when it comes from a sincere and selfless heart.

When you are in love, you feel on top of the world, it brings you joy and excitement. Bringing it to where you are in your relationship with this person you've been spending time with, you now need to determine whether you are in love with this person or not. If that person has captivated your heart even more, if you find yourself thinking about him or her with joy when they are not with you, if you can't wait to see that person again when you are not together, if you find yourself thinking often of that person, if you become lost in long conversations without realizing how much time has passed, and if you don't want your conversation, date, or meeting to end because you're already missing that person, then you are in love!

> As your relationship grows and evolves, so will your love for each other, and you need to continue to nurture that love by staying connected.

As your relationship grows and evolves, so will your love for each other, and you need to continue to nurture that love by staying connected. At some point in time, you will naturally start expressing your love for one another. While your feelings for each other grow stronger, do not get carried away. There is still work to do. You can't completely know a person in even a year. As a matter of fact, human beings are always evolving. Just when you think you known a person, they can change as they go through different phases in life, and this is the same for you. The message here is that you should keep learning more about each other.

At this stage of your relationship, you both need to determine what's next. Nothing should be left to chance, and for a Christian, please avoid "going with the flow." There is a danger zone of indecisiveness, time wasting, and setting up for failure in this stage. The Bible says, "Where there is no vision, people perish" (Proverbs 29:18). This scripture is very clear and applying it to the context of relationships without goals or vision will lead nowhere but heartaches and frustration.

Be intentional about your relationship; assess where you are and where you want to be. You initially met and made your intentions known to the other. You discussed your goals and purpose for dating. Then you agreed that you want to give it a shot. Now, you've come to a point where you've gotten to know each other well enough to determine that you love one another that you want to make a commitment to proceed to courtship. Therefore, the next step is to be open with each other about how you feel. I really can't determine or estimate the timing on how long this should take or when it should happen because every relationship is unique. The two people involved can determine the best timing for this conversation to happen.

The beauty of any relationship lies in the flexibility of the people involved and their ability to let things happen naturally without any pressures of a preset timeline. Let your relationship grow steadily so that you can enjoy every moment of it. Focus on the process and the person you are with rather than following other people's unrealistic expectations or some social timeline you found on Google or social media.

I mention this timeline because there exists a general relationship timeline that most people tend to go by. Such a timeline usually includes when to have your first kiss, when to say I love you, and how long you should know each other before making a commitment to be in a relationship. I plead with you to let the Lord direct you and set your own rules for your budding relationship.

The simple truth is that every relationship is so unique that it cannot be predicted by any preset rule. Who sets those rules anyway? There are trends people tend to follow without verifying or authenticating how they originated. There is danger in trying to conform your perfectly growing relationship to meet some societal standard and thereby straining it. We tend to care too much about what people think and how people will view us and our relationships that we try to fit it to some pre-framed picture of perfection.

But God does not work according to human expectations or preset rules and expectations. *"For my thoughts are not your thoughts, neither are my ways your ways, declares the Lord"* (Isaiah 55:8). Forcing your relationship to comply with worldly standards would only disrupt the work of God. I hereby encourage you to let your relationship flow as smoothly and naturally as possible without forcing anything. Remain intentional about your goals and follow the leading of the Holy Spirit.

Considering how far you've come in relating with this special person in your life, you should know the person well enough to decide whether he or she is the kind of person you want to be with or not.

In deciding whether or not to proceed in the journey of love or not, be honest with yourself without making excuses for anything. If you don't see your relationship going anywhere and if you feel nothing for this other person for some time, please do each other the favor of expressing how you feel in a nice and polite way. Ensure that you are being sensitive and considerate of the person while expressing that you are not interested in committing to a relationship with them.

In some cases, one person is more interested than the other person, but the Bible makes it clear by asking "can two walk together unless they agree?" (Amos 3:3). It may be necessary to define your level of interaction and set boundaries. If the feeling is mutual, you can agree on how you want to define your friendship. In some cases, long lasting friendships come out of this phase, and that's why it's important to build that friendship. Regardless, if you are going to move forward, you need to learn more about that person's character.

However, if you've built your friendship to a point where you both desire to be together, have a heart-to-heart conversation to review your relationship. Have a conversation about each other, what you love about one another, how much you enjoy each other's company, and what your intentions are for one another. If you are a guy, state your intention and feelings about how much you love the girl. Yes, now you can tell how much you cherish her and she you.

Do a pulse check: are you now more comfortable with each other, open to sharing more about yourselves? If so, it will feel like you've known each other for decades. You need to be intentional about your relationship as you proceed to take your relationship to the next level. This is where you commonly hear people say, "Let's make it official," meaning to let people know you are in a relationship, such as on social media, for example. While some people at this stage might be comfortable letting their loved ones and friends know, some might decide to keep it to themselves, but the main point is that they are committing to being in a relationship as boyfriend and girlfriend.

This phase is the beginning of something new. Everything you've done before now was preparation, and recall, every stage is a preparation for the next. There is often a misconception that being in a committed relationship of boyfriend and girlfriend is the *final* destination. This is not true. When you believe you've reached your destination, you stop taking action, you stop growing. You basically relax, which can be detrimental to the longevity and sustainability of such a relationship.

You need to spend time together and talk about your goals for your relationship. The goals and intentions you had at the beginning of the relationship can now be broken down in pieces and needs to be mapped out or aligned. Each of you have your individual goals for your life, career, education, and so on. You will need to talk about these, because you must continue to work on your personal goals while building your relationships.

> Don't make someone else's relationship or some social expectations the standard for your relationship.

Often, people put their lives on hold for a relationship, and if they live in different states or countries, they will take time from their lives to visit each other. And this is the stage some couples will decide to set a timeline toward marriage. It is often under three years, all depending on the couple and other factors of consideration. That's why you need to talk, plan, and set goals.

No two relationships are exactly the same, and what works for one might not necessarily work for another. This is why it's important to define your own relationship as it works for both of you. Don't make someone else's relationship or some social expectations the standard for your relationship. This book doesn't have any special secret formula. Instead, it serves as a guide to help you discern the right path and to help you keep in mind some key principles as you walk your relationship journey.

Nevertheless, remember to always keep God at the center, and the Holy Spirit will teach you what to do at all times. You have a chance to create something beautiful out of your relationship, and unless you have a sketch or rough draft of what you're looking to build, it might be difficult to obtain that masterpiece you desire.

Chapter Six Questions

1. What have you learned about courtship?

2. What is your plan or goal toward courtship?

3. If you are currently in a relationship, are you in the courtship phase without realizing it? If so, what will you start doing differently?

4. What has been your experience in courtship? Have you been intentional about it?

CHAPTER SEVEN
Courtship Phase: The Dos and Don'ts of Courtship

As you proceed in your commitment to each other toward marriage in God's will, keep in mind that everything you do and the relationship you are building is what will eventually become a marriage. As a married woman now, I can tell you from the other side that the friendship, love, differences, problems, and everything you have at the dating and courtship stage will not disappear and be completely different after marriage.

Whatever you build now is what will transition into a marriage. Marriage will not change anything about your relationship; it will only magnify what you have or give you room to build upon your dating foundation. This is why it is important to build with

> *Marriage will not change anything about your relationship; it will only magnify what you have.*

intentionality and seriousness. Nothing about a relationship should be left to chance. This chapter will therefore guide you on some things you should consider doing and not doing while building your relationship and the reasons behind each of these points to bring more enlightenment.

Grow Together Spiritually

Make prayer the foundation of your relationship. Never forget that your relationship is unique and not the same as any other relationship out there. A Christian relationship should always reflect Christian values and should not be defined by societal standards or social expectations. Let God always be the glue that keeps you bound together. Share your spiritual journey with each other. The most beautiful thing about being a Christian is the oneness in Spirit. The Spirit of the Lord that lives in both of you will connect you more than anything else and becomes your fueling ground.

The Bible states in Ephesians 4:1, "Make every effort to keep the unity of the Spirit through the bond of peace." You should consider having a common spiritual practice as a way to continue to grow your spiritual lives as a couple. I have a close friend who once told me that when she and her husband were courting prior to marriage, they would pray together every morning before heading to work. Praying should not be a chore. This is your sacred place, and if your eventual goal is to be married, you will want to handle your relationship with care and every aspect of it intentionally.

Take Time to Build a Healthy Relationship

As you're building your relationship, you are walking life's journey together. It is important to communicate regularly because that's the best way to know more about your personalities, likes, dislikes, goals, aspirations, and more. This is the phase where you need to create space in each other's lives for one another. You would naturally find yourselves having some kind of routine, like working out together, playing games, reading books, going out to eat, or enjoying fun activities together. Your friendship can never be taken away from you and is a strong bond you can and should take time to build upon.

Pay Attention to Each Other's Character

I gave an analogy earlier in this book of viewing every stage in a relationship as layers of onions that are peeled off, one after the other. As you build your relationship, you will undoubtedly discover more about each other's character. Ensure you are paying close attention to each other to identify all you need to know about and further determine if you can walk the journey of life together.

Work on Your Goals Together

The reason why you need to talk about your goals is because every single person on this planet is created for a purpose and we ought to each fulfill that purpose. Hence, each person in the relationship ought to have both short-term and long-term goals in life. If you've identified a person you can potentially spend the rest of your life with, you should be able to discuss those goals. A relationship should not be a hindrance to the fulfillment of your purpose. Therefore, you should be able to work together, supporting one another and working toward achieving your individual goals. Using the biblical term, you should be "helping" each other to fulfill your destiny and propose.

Grow Together in Love and Nurture Your Love

As mentioned in chapter six, taking time to grow together in love is essential to the sustainability of your relationship. Commit the attributes of love described in 1 Corinthians 13 to your heart, making sure you and your partner are working to reflect each in your relationship.

Also, remember the second and greatest commandment as stated in Matthew 22:39, "You shall love your neighbor as yourselves." To make this scripture more relatable and practical, you must think about how you love yourself and just project it to your partner...assuming you are loving as God has commanded. Hopefully, you truly love yourself, otherwise it will be disastrous for any relationship because you cannot give what you don't have. However, if you love God as stated in verse 38 of Matthew 22, you should not find it difficult to love yourself and love your neighbor.

When you each have the mindset to love as Christ has asked us to love, your relationship will be peaceful and joyful to the extent that it can be described as heaven on earth. While God can give you what you desire for your life and relationship, the work is left in your hand to do. In this instance, it is for you to nurture your love and let it blossom over time.

Having discussed some of the things you should do in relationships, the next section will describe what you should avoid doing and why.

Don't Let Your Partner Take the Place of God

When you are in love, it is very easy to quickly drift to the point of making everything in your life about your partner. However, this isn't God's plan for you. He stated in Genesis 2 that He wants to make help suitable for the man, but I don't think God's intention was to replace Himself with Eve in the life of Adam. Be therefore careful to maintain your spiritual life by keeping a strong relationship with God. Your partner should respect that in you, and you should respect it in them.

If you've always served in the ushering department of your church or if you have a routine service to God, do not let your relationship affect your commitment. Bear this in mind: anytime your ministry or connection with God dwindles as a result of you creating more time for your relationship, you are beginning to make that person and relationship your god. This is perhaps the thing God does not like the most as stated in Exodus 3:14, "Do not worship any other god, for the Lord, whose name is Jealous, is a jealous God."

Don't Make Your Partner the Main Source of Your Happiness

Another instance in which you shouldn't let your partner take the place of God is not to expect them to be your main source of happiness. While they can contribute to your level of happiness, please be intentional about not placing your happiness in the hands of another person, including the love of your life.

In my previous relationships prior to getting married, I sought for human love and affection that I thought was going to bring about happiness, but it was never enough to fill my soul. I was frustrated and sometimes unhappy because I thought a relationship was supposed to bring me happiness. However, I later learned that no human is equipped to make anyone happy or capable enough to love the way we want to be loved. Even now, in marriage, I have come to terms with God being the major source of life, love, hope, peace, and joy that can sustain me through the blissful and tough times. This is a major reason why starting with God is crucial before even thinking of dating. This level of happiness comes with being whole in your singleness. Let God be the source of your happiness and be determined to be always in control of your happiness.

Avoid Having Sex

Sex is God's gift to humans, and it is good. However, while it is good, it is not just created for fun, exploration, or to be used as a tool of manipulation to get what we want, including love and relationship sustenance or security.

There is usually this school of thought that the reason why young people are told to avoid sex while dating is only about virginity, but I want to let you know that it's much more than being about virginity. It's about purity, clarity, sacredness, and basically about avoiding sin. If sex before marriage were only tied to virginity, people who have had sex before will find it difficult to see a reason why they should avoid sex in the future.

According to the Word of God in 1 Corinthians 7:1-2, "*It is* good for a man not to touch a woman. Nevertheless, because of sexual immorality, let each man have his own wife, and let each woman have her own husband." Sex outside marriage has become so normalized that we Christians are also caught in this web of doing it because everyone else is doing it. The pleasure derived from sex can be gratifying for the moment, but the feeling is only temporary, and soon after, you will want more. It's easy to say, "Well, I'm eighteen, I'm an adult, and I can do whatever I want and sleep with whomever I want." You are completely right as far as the world goes, but this should not be the mindset of a Christian. As a Christian, you've made a commitment to do things God's way, renouncing sin and worldly desires which is the major reason to avoid sex.

I acknowledge that it might be hard to abstain from sex when you've found someone you love and have been spending time with him or her, but if you both make a commitment to each other and make the decision as Christians to be celibate, you can do it. The problem usually arises when only one person has decided to be celibate and the other does not agree or want to be understanding. This alone is enough reason to know that you should not be with such a person.

If you ever find yourself in a relationship that makes you compromise on your commitment to God, your personal values, and everything you believe in, you will need to decide to either stay and make it about you and the relationship or end it to focus more on God. Yes, it might be painful, it might be hard, you may really love that person, but please know that whenever you compromise, you are losing a part of you, denying God, and releasing yourself to be manipulated by the devil.

This was exactly what Eve did. She compromised, she agreed that it wouldn't hurt to try it, she agreed that God's Word didn't matter at that point, she lost herself for a second, and everything changed (Genesis 3). The consequences that come for Christians who compromise on things that seem mundane are far greater than the act itself. Other people might not suffer the consequences the way you will, but this sin is you cheating on God, disregarding God, and choosing to satisfy yourself and give yourself to a human being out of God's will. This is not pleasing to God.

Additionally, enumerated below are several other reasons why you should avoid sex:

Your Body Is the Temple of God

The Bible says in 1 Corinthians 6:18-20, "Flee sexual immorality. Every sin that a man does is outside the body, but he who commits sexual immorality sins against his own body. Or do you not know that your body is the temple of the Holy Spirit *who is* in you, whom you have from God, and you are not your own? For you were bought at a price; therefore glorify God in your body and in your spirit, which are God's."

This Bible text expressly states that your body belongs to God and not to you. As a result, you should not do as you please to it, but everything you do with your body should bring glory to Him. Imagine how the temple of the Lord is! It is a sacred place, a place of reverence and holiness. Begin to view and handle your body as such! Also note, that you will eventually get married, so you will have plenty of opportunity to enjoy sexual pleasure as you desire.

It Conflicts with the Holy Spirit

Galatians 5:17 says, "For the flesh lusts against the Spirit, and the Spirit against the flesh; and these are contrary to one another, so that you do not do the things that you wish." According to this Bible verse, the body seems to always be at war with the Holy Spirit. You must be aware of this so that you may have plans in place to overcome the flesh. The battle ground for this is your mind. Whenever you allow lustful thoughts and desires to creep in, you begin to ruminate on it, which is where your body starts coming up with excuses and reasons why you should do it while the Holy Spirit is warning you against it at the same time. The Bible text states that when this happens, you won't do the things you want to do; it implies the following and more:

- o It confuses you and makes it difficult to discern what is right.

- o It clouds your judgment. It can make you unnecessarily attached to the wrong person and make it difficult to break up even when there is a need to.

- o It makes you lose focus.

It's Not the Right Time

"I charge you, O daughters of Jerusalem, By the gazelles or by the does of the field, Do not stir up nor awaken love until it pleases" (Song of Solomon 2:7). This Bible text is straight forward, indicating the need to wait till the time is right to do it with the right person in marriage. Stirring up love before its time is like opening Pandora's box.

It Can Devalue the Relationship

Some relationships have broken up because sex was constantly used to sustain the relationship without the other foundational basis discussed earlier. Sex will not sustain a relationship. Though it might seem sweet at some point, it is not love.

You Will Confuse Lust for Love

Sex is one way to express love when married. It is also God's intent for procreation. However, sex outside of marriage is fornication. In such a situation, it doesn't matter how pleasurable you believe sex is as a single person or you believe it to be as an adult. You might be having sex whenever you live with someone you are in love with. Regardless, it is not complete or appropriate until after marriage.

> Sex will not sustain a relationship. Though it might seem sweet at some point, it is not love.

Pregnancy

You have heard that one of God's intentions for sex is procreation and this is part of two people becoming one in marriage. "For this reason, a man shall leave his father and his mother, and be joined to his wife; and they shall become one flesh. And the man and his wife were both naked and were not ashamed" (Genesis 2:24-25).

The biblical and physical reality of sex is that it can lead to pregnancy, and though science has developed birth control options, it still doesn't provide 100% guarantee of pregnancy prevention. Meaning, that every time there is a heterosexual sexual interaction, there is always a chance of it resulting in pregnancy, and once that happens, there are life changing decisions to be made.

Such decisions can include if you should or should not have an abortion, making a sacrifice to put the baby up for adoption, changing your life's plans to prioritize the baby, and so on. The possible ripple effect of having sex outside marriage far outweighs the short-lived pleasure derived from it. It is therefore more advisable to wait for the right time to have sexual intercourse appropriately and endlessly if you so wish when married.

What If I'm Already Having Sex?

If you are already having sex, stop! "There is therefore now no condemnation to those who are in Christ Jesus, who do not walk according to the flesh, but according to the Spirit" (Romans 8:1). You may have had sex in a previous relationship or current relationship but the great thing about Christianity is that we have been redeemed by the blood of the Lamb! The Lord requires us to renounce sin, put off our old ways, and become new in Christ. Old things shall pass away, and all things become new (2 Corinthians 5:17). This means that you can stop having sex now and focus on more important things in your relationship.

I have heard of people having sexual intercourse when they would have otherwise waited because they feared losing their relationship. If the other person is going to break up with you simply because you don't want to have sex, then that man or woman is not right for you. If, however, he or she disagrees but is willing to respect your decision, you may proceed with caution and be ready to put in the work of exercising self-control and pulling the brakes before you fall back into the old ways.

If you and the person you are with have known each other well enough, are Christians, are mature enough, are financially independent, and have mutual understanding of staying committed to one another and would like to continue having sex, then get married. You can review the steps discussed earlier in this book and ensure you can see the evidence in your relationship to go toward marriage. The Apostle Paul makes it clear in 1 Corinthians 7:9 that if you cannot abstain from sex, you should get married.

I would, however, like to caution you to make sure you are not getting married for the sole reason of having sex. Doing so is dangerous to the sustainability of your marriage because other factors come into play. So, the question now is: how can you avoid sex when you've found someone you are head over heels in love with and you know you it might lead to marriage?

How to Avoid Sex

Walk in the Spirit. Stay connected to God as spiritual alertness makes it possible to reject sin. "So I say, walk by the Spirit, and you will not gratify the desires of the flesh" (Galatians 5:16).

Avoid living together before getting married. This topic has come up and been debated on a few occasions. The question is: what is your major purpose for living together? If you are dating and each of you have your own place to stay and decide to live together because you want to be closer to each other, then why is marriage out of that equation? This is exactly what people who decide to get married do after marriage. In some cases, couples might start planning their wedding, and depending on where they live, they might move in together. In such cases, both should have parental consent if applicable. In this case, you would need to determine how to avoid fornication. Deciding to live together for no solid reason besides the fact that you're dating and in love is not enough reason. Please apply wisdom and beware of falling into sin and making sin a lifestyle.

Get an accountability partner or join a celibacy group. There is power in accountability, especially in the body of Christ. The same way peer pressure influences people to do what they don't want to do, so can a positive support group help you toward achieving the desired outcome. I believe being in an environment, group, or having an accountability partner with similar focus will make a difference. There are celibacy groups you can join if you choose, or you can start one in your own circle of friends and local church.

Plan ahead on how to handle temptation. Agree on a gameplan and determine what you would do if both feel tempted to have sex.

> *Therefore, I encourage you to determine how to approach your relationship in a way that brings glory to God.*

Would you both need to take a walk outside, play games, have a warning code, or would the other person need to go home? No matter what, please don't underestimate the power of temptation. A whole line in the Lord's prayer says, "Lead us not into temptation" (Matthew 6:13). It is advisable to be watchful and careful not to fall into temptation, but more importantly, you need to plan on how to handle temptation. One way is to flee sexual immorality (1 Corinthians 6:18). If you recall Joseph's story, he had to flee Potiphar's wife after she kept tempting him. He had refused several advances, but she wouldn't stop, so he had to flee when things were about to get out of hand (Genesis 39:12).

"For this is the will of God, your sanctification: that you abstain from sexual immorality; that each one of you know how to control his own body in holiness and honor, not in the passion of lust like the Gentiles who do not know God; that no one transgress and wrong his brother in this matter, because the Lord is an avenger in all these things, as we told you beforehand and solemnly warned you. For God has not called us for impurity, but in holiness. Therefore whoever disregards this, disregards not man but God, who gives his Holy Spirit to you" (1 Thessalonians 4:3-8).

Therefore, I encourage you to determine how to approach your relationship in a way that brings glory to God. As you proceed in a relationship, be spiritually and physically alert, discerning what is right, holy, and acceptable to the Lord. I pray that the Lord will guide you and direct every action you take in your relationship.

Chapter Seven Questions

1. What have you learned from this chapter?

2. What would you start doing differently based on the content of this chapter?

3. How do you plan to build your relationship?

4. What are your views about sex in a relationship other than marriage?

5. What would you do to maintain sexual purity in your relationship?

6. What are your relationship dos and don'ts? (This will help to know what you can't compromise on.)

7. If you are currently in a relationship, what conversations do you need to have with your partner to improve your relationship?

CHAPTER EIGHT
Courtship Phase: Relationship Reality

This chapter will discuss the reality of relationship or courtship in the right context—after the butterflies settle and you no longer see each other as strangers. At this stage, you should be quite comfortable with each other, almost like friends who deal with everyday life and the dynamics of relationships, including working together and handling disagreements. To that end, this chapter will highlight the realities of a growing relationship, particularly some of the problems that arise in relationships and how to address them.

In economics, there is a concept known as diminishing returns. It alludes to the effect where profits or benefits gained from something will proportionally decrease as more money or energy is

While some things can change about a person over time, there is also a possibility that some things will never change.

invested in it. Something similar happens in your dating relationship. The more you spend time with one another and get to know more about each other the more you become comfortable around them. The adrenaline rush may no longer be a rush. The butterflies will no longer bother you. Your relationship becomes "normalized" in the way you feel. It's easy to think that your feelings have decreased. Some people even conclude that this means they are no longer in love. This isn't necessarily true, which is the reason why I mentioned in chapter six that love is not a feeling. If it was only a feeling, you will find it difficult to keep a relationship or become frustrated when your feeling is not sustainable at the same level you initially felt.

As we explore this topic further in this chapter, I hope this guides you in assessing yourself and how this might have occurred in any previous relationships, if you've been in any. I commonly hear, "I just don't feel it anymore. I am not connected to this person. The excitement is not there anymore. The butterflies have disappeared." Such sayings show that love is being evaluated as a feeling. This feeling-oriented mindset will reveal the true depth of your love. Emotionally dependent people will find this very difficult to handle because they will always be looking for that feeling.

But for almost everything in life, the law of diminishing returns applies. For example, when I was growing up, my parents often bought us snacks that we enjoyed. When we first discovered a treat, such as Twinkies, we would eat them all the time, but after a while, we begin losing the intense desire for them. The same thing can happen after you've become more familiar with a person, and this is why you must have a stronger basis for connection other than just feelings.

So, as you get to know your girlfriend or boyfriend closely, you may come into conflict with each other. In such instances, pay attention to the way you both deal with conflicts and determine how to best tackle issues as a couple. This is paramount to the growth of your relationship. This stage requires your full attention to make sure you are with the right person and the relationship is adding value to both parties and glorifying God. I encourage you to make it a priority to always keep God in the equation. He is the x-factor in your algebraic equation.

At this stage, continue to relate with one another, grow together, and know each more in depth. This will regularly confirm or question why you are made for each other. You should be honest with yourself as you get to know the other person. Ask yourself: is this the person I would like to spend the rest of my life with? This singular question will guide you in determining what you want and what is good for you. There is no need to leave everything to time and chance, especially when you are leaning toward dissatisfaction with the person you're with. It is important to seize the time in order to make an informed decision. God has given us that ability to see, identify, accept, and reject things. All He did in Genesis 2 was to present the woman to Adam. God didn't say anything thereafter. Adam and Eve were then in control from that point on. However, they were still accountable to God. If, at any point in time, you and your boyfriend or girlfriend lose sight of the fact that God is part of your relationship, you are heading in the wrong direction—which is a recipe for disaster.

Determine what you can and cannot stand about the other person. This is a critical and honest evaluation you must carry out. I have seen many couples overlook certain things that annoy them about their boyfriend or girlfriend, hoping they will change some day. In actual sense, there is really nothing wrong with overlooking those things if that's your choice, but the problem comes when you truly cannot overlook them. In that situation, what you are doing is building resentment that will eventually negatively impact the relationship.

While some things can change about a person over time, there is also a possibility that some things will never change. The major question now is: if the things you don't like about this person never change, do you have the bandwidth to accept it and not be bothered by it? Remember the law of diminishing returns. As you get to know each other, time reveals the good, bad, and ugly of this person you are in love with, and if you are not being candid with yourself about what you can deal with or not handle, you are going to reach an uncontainable breaking point. What then would you need to do to address this? You can start by communicating with each other.

> *Relationships require communication to grow, thrive, and survive.*

Relationships require communication to grow, thrive, and survive. The word "relationship" indicates the need to relate. Far too often, I have seen couples who refuse to communicate yet expect significant changes in their relationships. I have also found myself in a situation where I expected my partner to know what I disliked and when no change occurred or he remained oblivious to the problem, I became frustrated, moody, and irritable, leaving him confused and trying to figure out what's wrong with me. We are human beings who see things in different ways, and we can't expect others to be mind-readers.

The major problem with this kind of mindset is that you assume the other person sees what you are seeing as a problem, but they might not. If I have a habit that's become a part of me for many years, I might never see any issue with it. So, the person who does see it as an issue has an obligation to communicate their concerns so there can be a discussion about it. In some of these instances, the other person might be offended and defensive, thinking there is nothing wrong even after it has been communicated. This is where miscommunication and conflicts start building up in relationships. I urge you to apply wisdom in your relationships, wisdom to support growth and change rather than being demanding and trying to force the change.

Trying to make someone be what you want them to be, when you want them to, and how you want them to is a selfish, controlling, and abusive way to approach a relationship. It will not work. Instead, it will only create a hostile and toxic environment. This is how a sweet relationship gradually becomes toxic. I believe a relationship is an opportunity to grow along with someone else with respect for individuality. In other words, no one owns anybody. This also applies to marriage. In marriage, we are just choosing to walk this journey of life together and we should allow each other to be the person we were created to be while helping one another improve on our weaknesses. Therefore, I encourage you to communicate and express your concern about a particular habit you don't like with love.

Start with a compliment. Follow that with how much you want to support him or her to be the best version of themselves. Only then state your observation and how it makes you feel. Many people struggle with communicating their concerns and since nothing changes, they find they can no longer tolerate certain things which eventually leads to a breakup. I have seen relationships that end abruptly without explanations or communication. This is not good.

We are relational beings, and we ought to communicate effectively to gain understanding and learn ways to grow.

The first thing to do is to communicate. Next, you must allow time for change. If a person has been doing things a certain way for years, they won't be able to change it in a few months. In all honesty, while there might be a measure of change, it might not meet your expectations. You should determine what you can accept or not. Some people make life too difficult by demanding a certain type or degree of change they want, but this results in resistance and resentment from the other person if they are not open to it. A lady once shared a few concerns she had about her boyfriend, such as improving communication skills and doing things in a certain way that she thought was more proper. I then asked if he acknowledged that these were issues. Was he willing to change, and was the lady willing to give him enough time to change? If this man has done a certain thing for 30 years, he won't change quickly. She acknowledged that he was trying to improve and decided she needed to give him more time to continue to improve.

The third step is to determine how important this issue is to you and your relationship. Is it a deal breaker? In truth, you can't really control what you like and don't like. So, the question is: can you tolerate it? If your answer is no, then be honest with yourself and with the person you are with and determine if you want to proceed with your relationship. While being honest, also bear in mind that no one is perfect, and everyone has their strengths and weaknesses. So, when thinking about relationships, weigh things on a scale of weaknesses versus strengths. Do some of their strengths outweigh their weaknesses? No one can determine these things for you, but what you need to do is to assess the situation, the person, your relationship with them, how much you love them, and how much you want this person in your life irrespective of their weaknesses.

This stage is a real eye opener to the world of marriage which can simply be defined as the union of two people who have agreed to walk the journey of life together, accepting each other as they are. The lady mentioned in the previous paragraph was hoping her relationship of about a year would end up in marriage, but she still had concerns. I had her ask some reality check questions:

➢ Do you love this person and believe he or she also genuinely loves you?

➢ Are you willing to be patient with him or her and give them a chance to change at their own pace and will?

➢ Do you love the person enough to accept those annoying things about them even if they don't change?

➢ Are your concerns deal breakers? In order words, would these make you end the relationship if they don't change?

➢ How would you handle those situations or those things about them?

These were questions she had to go think about to determine if the relationship was worth continuing. While it is great to be considerate of your partner, you also need to be honest about what you can tolerate and not tolerate. These are decisions that cannot be made for you or by anyone else. It requires deep soul searching and the ability to make sound decisions.

Problems in Relationships

Problems arise in relationships for various reasons, such as when the couple find it difficult to work out their differences, when there is no respect for one another, when there are unspoken expectations, when one person is trying to change the other, when there is lack of communication and understanding, and so on.

Lack of Communication or Poor Communication

One of the major points you should note from this chapter is that the survival of every relationship *strongly* depends on communication. Without communication, your relationship would have never started. Even the Bible confirms that two cannot walk together unless they agree (Amos 3:3).

Solution: I strongly encourage you to find a way to work on your communication skills. If this is your weakness, learn more about how to communicate better by reading books and watching video teachings on it. Don't expect the people around you to simply accept this aspect of your personality. You will only frustrate anyone you end up being with. If two poor communicators meet, can any good relationship grow between them? I don't think so...unless they devise a communication strategy that works for them. While you don't have to be a perfect communicator, you must be willing to talk to your partner and reach an understanding. That's the basic requirement and purpose of communication.

> *If two poor communicators meet, can any good relationship grow between them?*

Unspoken Expectations Breed Frustration and Resentment

Let's get practical here. If your boyfriend or girlfriend doesn't express their feelings and you value words of affirmation as your love language, this can be quite frustrating for you. This is where the real work and challenges are in relationships. No matter how alike two people are, they will never be the same. So, the real work lies in a couple's ability to work through each other's differences.

In this situation, there is more than one problem. First, there are the differences between the two people: one person likes words of affirmation and the other doesn't express feelings. Second is the expectation that the other person should know and consistently express words of affirmation. Third is the lack of understanding and acknowledging the differences in personality and the approach to things. All these issues build frustration, resentment, and disagreements.

Solution:

> **Express your expectation.** Don't forget, we are only human and not mind readers. You will only get results when you make a request and state problems.

> **Be realistic.** Have realistic expectations that your partner can easily meet.

> **Be understanding.** Recognize and respect each other's differences, which leads to better understanding. Here is a major way to address differences: knowing each other's capacity and acknowledging when a person is not wired to meet your expectations.

> **Be flexible.** Give the other person the flexibility to meet your expectation in their own time and at their own pace.

Not Accepting Individual Differences

Research has shown irreconcilable differences as one of the reasons why people divorce. I personally don't think that the differences are the major issue at heart here. I believe it is the ability to accept or to handle the differences and then to work together despite the differences.

➤ **Accept and tolerate** each other's differences. If you can't accept it, please do everybody a favor, and discontinue the relationship.

➤ **Make plans** on how to work around those differences.

➤ **Agree to disagree.** Decide to not argue about your point or preference.

Trying to Change a Person and Demanding the Change Immediately

The differences between a couple are not always the major problem but how they manage and address these differences. The problem arises when one person believes their way is the best and the other must change to adapt to their expectations. This kind of thought actually reflects a hint of pride. Only a proud person thinks their way is the best and someone must be like them. It's actually a subtle way of presenting yourself as a god and this is not Christianly. Be careful to avoid getting to the point where you are demanding a person to be what you want them to be.

Solution:

➤ Your duty as a Christian is to point that person back to God by praying about it or reading the Word of God.

➤ Acknowledge and accept each other's differences.

➤ Be tolerant. Determine whether you can tolerate the identified difference. If you can't, please do each other a favor by discontinuing the relationship. Tolerance is a person's willingness to accept other habits, views, and opinions different from their own.

➤ Communication.

➤ Patience.

Seeking Perfection

Dear reader, please note that perfection is an illusion, and any effort you make to obtain it will be futile. Do yourself a favor and save yourself from frustration by accepting that perfection doesn't exist on earth. Only God is perfect, but we can always pray as David did in Psalm 138:8 that "The Lord will perfect *that which* concerns me." Rather than seeking perfection, learn to acknowledge improvements and celebrate progress while moving toward more improvements.

Finally, I encourage you to reflect on the content of this chapter and identify what you would like to improve based on your self-assessment and experience from past relationships. Working on your mindset and how you contribute to problems in relationships will only prepare you for a healthier relationship in the future.

Chapter Eight Questions

1. What are your major takeaways from this chapter?

2. What have you learned about yourself based on the content of this chapter?

3. What have you realized about your relationship trends if you've been in previous relationships?

4. If you are currently in a relationship, what are you realizing about yourself, your boyfriend or girlfriend, and the way you handle your relationship?

5. What would you do differently going forward?

CHAPTER NINE
Assessment Phase: Break Up or Move Forward?

In life, all conclusions are based on some sort of assessment or evaluation. While this seems like an academic theory, it was first a biblical principle initiated by God. The Bible tells us in Genesis chapters 1 and 2 that God created everything, and after each creation, He saw that it was good. For example, Genesis 1:31 states that God saw all that he had made, and it was very good. And there was evening, and there was morning—the sixth day. That right there shows that God did the work, evaluated His work, validated it, and concluded that it was good. Similarly, I believe an assessment was made to conclude that Adam needed a suitable helper in Genesis 2:18 which states, "The Lord God said, 'It is not

The evaluation of a relationship can and will sometimes lead to a breakup or marriage and this process should not be ignored.

good for the man to be alone. I will make a helper suitable for him.'" That is the power of evaluation.

There is always a need for evaluation. I had a habit of assessing what's going well and what needs to improve before I got married. I do this in marriage now, too. This can also be a good practice for you if you choose to do it. I was once in a relationship where I had to assess if that was what I had envisioned for myself as an ideal relationship. I remember asking myself, "Is this the life I ordered?" The answer was already in the question, since there were things I was unhappy about, but I was trying so hard to make it work. It really wasn't what I wanted but it was hard for me to see it that way until I got to a point where critical self-reflection and assessment of the relationship was needed. It took a while for God to open my eyes and make me come to terms with the answer to that question.

I hereby encourage you to pay attention to how much God is involved in your life, how you invite Him into your situations, and the way you communicate with God and vice versa. I have learned that Christ leads us in our life's journey and walks hand in hand with us. He is in your thoughts, in your mind, and in your heart. You only need to stay attuned to Him. I am now realizing that when I assess the progress of a relationship, I am asking God questions. When you ask Him questions about your relationship, He will answer you clearly, but you need to listen and accept.

In some cases, you might find yourself asking questions you already know the answers to but are hoping God will give you a different answer, and when you don't get the answer you want, you conclude that God is not speaking to you. I believe God speaks to us all the time, but we tend to hit the mute button or turn in another direction from Him. As a Christian, identifying how God speaks to you is crucial to being led by Him, and your level of willingness to yield to His leading will determine the results you get. Assessing your relationship will help you determine what needs to improve and if it's worthwhile.

Adopting the habit of evaluating your life, relationships, environment, and everything God has placed around you is a good practice to ensure you are aligning with the purpose of God for your life. This chapter is to guide you in evaluating your relationship. Let's therefore explore further into assessing a relationship and how it should be done.

Why It Is Important to Evaluate

Assessing your relationship helps you to establish if it is working well and going as expected. Whenever you venture into anything, you have certain expectations, and you want to make sure after putting some work into it that the expected results are yielded or at least pointing in that direction. And if it's not working as expected, you can re-strategize by identifying what some of the issues are, what is not working, why it isn't working well, how it can be fixed, whether it's fixable or not, and what's next. The purpose of assessing something is to know if that thing is worthwhile. It is insane to embark on something without assessing to see if you are heading in the right direction. If you go too far without assessing, you run the risk of wasting your time and effort. Indeed, you might find it difficult to accept the reality of your situation even if you realize that it's not working.

How should this be done?

The way you go about assessing yourself is as important as the reason for doing it. You have to carefully determine on what basis you want to assess your relationship and carefully determine what your benchmark is.

I have seen couples get in the habit of comparing their relationships to other people's relationships as a way of benchmarking. This is a major mistake that can quickly destroy a relationship simply because other people's goals are different from yours. The common social media hashtag of the picture-perfect couples is *#relationshipgoals*. This means, when you see pictures or videos of a seemingly beautiful couple who are smiling, laughing, and doing fun things with each other, you start desiring that as your relationship goal. That becomes your benchmark in your relationship, which often becomes a point of contention when one person now has expectations the other does not. While there is nothing wrong with being inspired by other people's relationships, I advise you to be careful and avoid making other people's practices a major standard for your relationship, thereby putting a strain on yours. The two people in a relationship ought to define their own standard, discuss it, agree on it, and work on it as a couple based on individual and combined values and goals.

To assess your relationship, set aside time to think, both individually and as a couple. Ask these questions:

> ➤ Am I happy in this relationship?

> ➤ Do I love this person I'm with and does he or she love me in return?

> ➤ Does our relationship involve God and glorify him?

> ➤ Are we supporting each other well enough?

> ➤ Do we get along most of the time?

> ➤ Do we respect each other?

> ➤ Do we prioritize each other?

➢ Does my boyfriend or girlfriend truly care about my well-being and goals in life?

➢ Do we have a good relationship with each other's families?

➢ Is the relationship, as it stands now, what I want my marriage to be?

➢ Is this the person I want to spend the rest of my life with?

➢ Is this relationship what I envisioned for myself?

➢ Is it the will of God for us to get married?

The "Let Thy Will be Done" Prayer

In my opinion, praying for the will of God to be done in your life and relationship is a way to involve God in your assessment phase. This is one of the most difficult prayers to offer when you've already embarked on a journey because it might reroute you. However, it can also affirm God's approval.

Nevertheless, it is a prayer every Christian must learn to pray in any situation, including dating and courtship. I have been in a past relationship where I asked for the will of God to be done and I prayed for the strength to accept the outcome. God clearly made it known that the relationship wasn't His will, but I struggled letting go. However, this prayer allowed my mind to at least be open to letting God have His way. Eventually, the relationship ended.

A typical biblical example of this prayer was when Jesus was praying on the mountain before being arrested and crucified. He prayed for the cup to pass over Him if it pleased God but later resolved, "Not my will but thy will be done" (Luke 22:44). He was trying to negotiate with God, looking at the pain He would have to go through. While Jesus' situation is about death, the similarity here is important. It is the process of realizing God's will for your life and your willingness to accept it even when it will cause you pain. When I found myself praying for the will of God to be done before I got married, I would pray like this:

> *"Oh Lord, thank You for loving me. You knew me before I was formed in my mother's womb. Dear Lord, I pray for Your will to be done in my life, no matter how much I get in Your way. Please, give me the strength to accept the outcome of this prayer if it doesn't go my way. Amen."*

Praying this kind of prayer has helped me be more comfortable with submitting to the will of God. Learning to do the same will help you to trust God more. It also strengthens your relationship with God. Seeking for the will of God to be done in your life is an exercise of faith that you must be willing to undertake. If Jesus had not submitted to the will of God, the whole Kingdom's agenda to save us all would've been an aborted mission. In the same way, if you want a fulfilling, God-ordained relationship which will become a God-ordained marriage, you must learn to pray the "let thy will be done" prayer.

Make this part of your evaluation exercise. There is nothing more gratifying than having your relationship go through spiritual validation. What a privilege we have as children of God to carry everything to God in prayer.

Deciding to Break Up

The evaluation of a relationship can and will sometimes lead to either a breakup or marriage, and this process should not be ignored. If all your evidence or "signs" are pointing toward breaking up, please, in the name of Christ, do not ignore them. If it doesn't feel right, then it is not. Don't try to convince yourself otherwise. Many factors can play into that feeling, including not getting along well, not understanding each other, lack of respect for one another, not feeling loved, poor communication, misalignment of values, immaturity, and so on.

Don't be afraid to break up if a person or relationship is not aligning with God's purpose for your life. This is one of the ways God speaks to us, but we often ignore it, concluding that the problem is really not all that serious. Do not negotiate with the Holy Spirit. He speaks the truth, but He has left it to us to accept it or not. I acknowledge that the decision to break up is not always an easy one. Regardless of the reason behind it or how it eventually plays out, it requires serious and candid conversation with yourself to replay both the good and unpleasant aspects of your relationship before arriving at the conclusion to breakup. The sweet memories and other intimate bonds you've shared together will make it difficult. However, it must be done if you are convinced that the relationship is not God's will. When God shows you signs, you don't have to waste time negotiating.

You can have a direct conversation with your boyfriend or girlfriend. Give the other person the respect and courtesy of having an honest and empathetic conversation. If you are not too far from each other, make plans to meet up and discuss your concerns and decisions. If you don't live within the same city and there is absolutely no means of seeing each other soon, you can discuss the issue over the phone, using video calls.

Start by appreciating your relationship with them and explain why you believe the relationship should be discontinued. Give the other person a chance to respond. It might take time to process this, but with time, being clear about the boundaries you want to set will be helpful. You might think that it can't be that easy, and I agree that it is not easy to do, but again, as a child of God, you can also pray for God's guidance and help in discontinuing the relationship. "Is there anything too difficult for me?" says the Lord in Jeremiah 32:27. We don't invite God into our affairs enough, but when we do, He goes to work on our behalf. Unfortunately, some people tend to find a cowardly way out of relationships by "ghosting," ending all forms of communication without warning or explanation. This practice is very common as I've observed.

Discontinuing your relationship can be quite nerve-racking and as you do this, you ought to bear in mind that it took some time to build your relationship. Therefore, a breakup can be very painful, depending on how close you and your boyfriend or girlfriend have become and how long you've been together. I can, however, assure you that it will get better with time as long as you learn to accept that the relationship must end, and you gradually let go.

Accept that God has a plan for you if a relationship doesn't work out as you had hoped.

You determine how quickly you heal through acceptance and letting go. Learn to do things you enjoy, spend time with family and friends, get closer to God, get more involved in community activities, and so on. It is easy to become depressed following a breakup if you fail to accept the reality and find ways to get over the relationship. In such a case, no one can help you unless you make up your mind to let go and occupy yourself rather than brooding over a broken relationship. Accept that God has a plan for you if a relationship doesn't work out as you had hoped. "For I know the plans I have for you, declares the Lord, plans to prosper you and not harm you, plans to give you a hope and a future"

(Jeremiah 29:11). What great joy this assurance gives! His plans are not to harm you, even though a breakup might be painful. Remember that His Word says joy comes in the morning (Psalm 30:5). Therefore, let your heart be glad and take comfort in His words and rejoice in anticipation for what He will do.

Let's look on the bright side of a breakup. It is usually an opportunity to learn big life lessons. It helps to learn more about yourself, how to relate with the opposite sex, how to handle a relationship, what to do and avoid. Overall, it is a great growth opportunity, but if you fail to channel your break-up positively, you miss out on significant life lessons.

Questions to Guide Your Learning Process

Why did this relationship not work?
Regardless of how the breakup happened, I want to encourage you to accept that it has happened, whether you are at fault or not. The learning opportunity comes when you assess and identify the major problem that led to the breakup. Identifying why might help you find closure and learn how to address or avoid such situations in the future. However, in some instances, you might not be able to pinpoint a specific problem. Regardless, you can achieve a place of acceptance by believing God has better plans for you. If nothing else, let that be your closure.

What have I learned from this relationship?
Identify the good things you've learned, the bad things you need to avoid in the future, and the things you need to improve on. Every relationship teaches you about yourself, about others, and about life in general. When breakups occur, you need to learn your desires and expectations.

What do I need to learn about healthy relationships?

Identify what a healthy relationship is to you by identifying what was not so pleasant in the relationship. You might find yourself learning something you never knew before because of your experiences. You can learn from your behavior, the other person's behavior, and how you felt in the relationship (what made you sad, what made you happy).

How can I prepare for my next relationship based on lessons learned?

Make a plan on how you want to start working on those things you've identified as needing improvement. It could be how you handle money, how you talk, how you manage time, or hygiene. Imagine if people can divorce over something as silly as squeezing toothpaste in the middle and not from the bottom, it means there are always things to improve upon. You want to be mindful of anything you've learned about yourself. Now you would know what you can tolerate and can't tolerate.

The hard truth is that you might also realize that you are a little too uptight or too relaxed and need to make some adjustments to tolerate someone who isn't exactly like you. You can also decide that you want someone like you. The decision lies in your hands. The adjustments or improvements you decide to make in your life should prepare you better for the next phase in life. By the time you are done and are ready for the next one, you will be like refined gold.

In summary, this chapter has taught you the importance of evaluating your relationship, which is to affirm whether it is good enough to proceed with or if there is a need to discontinue. The guidelines are meant to steer you to view relationships through a spiritual lens yet opening your eyes to today's trends while choosing to tread the godly path to finding your God-given partner.

116

Romans 12:2 says, "Do not conform to the pattern of this world, but be transformed by the renewing of your mind. Then you will be able to test and approve what God's will is—his good, pleasing and perfect will."

Therefore, if you have decided to proceed with your relationship into marriage, the next chapter will guide you on what steps to take as you transition.

Chapter Nine Questions

1.   What is your major takeaway from this chapter?

2.   What are your thoughts about evaluation?

3.   What has your experience with evaluation been?

4.   How do you plan to assess your relationship now or in the future?

5.   Are you willing to make a sound decision with God's help after careful evaluation?

CHAPTER TEN
The Transitioning Phase (Becoming Engaged)

If you make it to the point of deciding to marry this person you've chosen by God's leading, it is worth celebrating. I congratulate you! You've been able to identify your God-given partner and have made the decision to accept them as such. If you recall in Genesis 2:22-23, God made Eve out of Adam's rib, then presented her to him, and when he saw her, he proclaimed, "This is now bone of my bone, and flesh of my flesh, she shall be called woman." This man identified his God-given partner and made a decision to accept her, and the Bible continued in verse 24 to state, "That is why a man leaves his father and mother and is united to his wife,

The relationship you are building is what will transition into marriage.

and they become one flesh." This chapter will cover how to transition into marriage.

Proceed into Marriage Intentionally

As mentioned in previous chapters, the relationship you are building is what will transition into marriage. You are already building your marital foundation. Getting married only certifies and legalizes it. Don't wait to get into marriage to start having serious talks. I have noticed from my single days and from mentoring other people about relationships that some important conversations are usually avoided before marriage. These things eventually become a source of disagreements and problems in marriage.

Only unserious or immature people avoid serious conversations. If you've decided to proceed into marriage, you should have very good knowledge of each other's finances. There should be no secrets you are hiding from each other. Your parents and families should know of your relationship. You should've talked about how you each respond to stress, how you each handle disagreements, and many more things.

Before deciding to get married, it is important to discuss your marital goals and expectations. If you've been open and relating well in your relationship, you would naturally have discussed your individual future goals and aspirations. You should already be leaning toward planning the future you desire together and trying to align your plans. If this has not been done prior to deciding to get married, it must be done as soon as possible before starting wedding preparations.

While you cannot figure out everything right from the onset, it is still very important to plan, discuss your plans, and agree on them. The Bible says that two cannot walk together unless they are agreed (Amos 3:3). Some of the important discussions you should have before getting married include but are not limited to the following:

> How many kids do you plan to have?

> Where will you live after getting married?

> How much do you each make?

> What are your fears about marriages?

> What are your expectations?

> How are you going to handle finances?

> How are you going to coordinate doing house chores?

> What kind of life do you desire?

Inform Your Families about Your Decision

The Apostle Paul said in Philippians 3:13, "Brothers and sisters, I do not consider myself yet to have taken hold of it." I urge you to do the same. Do not for any reason think you've got what you wanted and there is no need to keep working on your relationship. The real work has just begun in marriage.

You and your partner now have to continue the race of life together both spiritually and physically. See yourselves as a team running a marathon race. You both need to have a winning and team mindset to finish this race. Keep building your relationship in love and always remember to pray. Every time you pray, you are acknowledging God and activating His power in your lives and relationship. Keep this as a secret tool to always have in your marriage toolbox. Start building your marriage toolbox now. After all, if you're going on any journey, you plan and prepare by packing everything you think you will need on the trip. Marriage shouldn't be any different.

I acknowledge that some cultural practices vary when it comes to the right time to inform a family of a decision to marry. Once two people have decided to get married, it is up to them to determine the best time to inform the family. But in most cases, the man informs the bride's parents before proposing to the lady, which is also evident in the Bible, such as in the case of Jacob who went to ask Laban for Rachel's hand in marriage (Genesis 29:18). It's more or less asking for the parents' permission. It's then up to the groom to decide on the best time to propose. There is no set rule on how proposals should go. Again, there are cultural dynamics to this, and so it is advisable to follow your cultural requirements or preferences for proposing.

Get Spiritual Pre-Marital Counseling

Another major way to prepare for marriage is to go through structured "Christian" premarital counseling. Premarital counseling is very important for every Christian couple. It bewilders me to see some Christian couples go into marriage without premarital counseling. Counseling opens your eyes to the reality of marriage and starts preparing your mind for what you are about to get into.

I can tell you as a married person now that you can't be too prepared for marriage. Personally, premarital counseling put things in perspective for me with a lot of reality checks on my mindset. I am forever grateful for one of my pastor and his wife who counseled me and my husband based on biblical and personal experience. My husband and I are blessed to be surrounded by several spiritual mentors who prayed with us and counseled us.

Despite the butterflies in your belly and that head over heels in love feeling you're having, marriage is not always a bed of roses, and you have to be mentally prepared for it. One of the major lines of the Christian marital vow states, "In sickness and in health, for richer, for poorer, till death do us part." This simply means you stay together for life in good times and bad times. In truth, you can never know what curveballs life will throw at you but having that premarital counseling with a Spirit-led minister of God in addition to the foundation you've built together with God's help will prepare you for the journey ahead.

Marriage Is Not a Destination

As you plan your wedding, please bear in mind that marriage is not a destination. It is part of your life's journey in which you've decided to share with your God-given partner. I have seen people who believe that, once they are married, everything is complete with the fairytale line, "And they lived happily ever after." Most of those fairytale stories don't include the reality that exists after getting married. The work you put into your marriage will determine whether you'll live happily ever after or never after. Prepare your mind for marriage by accepting that the work begins from the first day of marriage. This is your opportunity at creating the amazing life you desire with the person you love, and this will not happen by chance.

Plan Your Wedding and Keep Learning

Planning your wedding is going to be the first major assignment you and your partner will work on together. Let me give you a quick reality check. There are couples who have broken up in the process of wedding planning. It is a big deal! This is one of the biggest days of your life, especially if you've dreamed of it for a long time. It is an important day in the bride and groom's life, and this needs to be understood on both sides. This is where your patience, love, respect, personality, and everything will be tested and shown.

Wedding planning is a phase where you would need to learn to communicate well, know more about each other's preferences, prioritize each other, and compromise. Remember, the wedding is for the bride and groom. In some cases, and cultures, parents and families also have influence on wedding planning decisions. This is where the main unit (the couple) needs to learn to be in agreement. Let your goal be to make sure you are all happy in the end. The couple needs to sit down and talk about what their dream wedding would look like. The bride shares and the groom shares, and then you decide on where compromise is needed, starting from the wedding colors to the venue, to the choice of music, to family involvement, and so on.

Set a wedding budget and discuss how the wedding will be funded. Decide if you need a wedding planner or not. If not, agree on how the wedding planning would be handled and how involved each of you will be in the process. Setup a time to discuss specifically the wedding. Set a wedding timeline and a to-do list. Nothing should be left to chance in your wedding planning process, just like in your marriage. Your attitude toward wedding planning will reflect a glimpse of your attitude toward your marriage. A person who chooses not to be involved in the wedding planning process at all might find it difficult to be actively involved in marriage. There are exceptions, such as those who are away on military duty or other unavoidable business or work trips. This also helps the other person in the relationship to determine if the level of involvement is what they want in a marriage.

Let's then get into the reasons why people breakup during the wedding planning. Some reasons include selfishness, poor communication, poor financial management mindset, and so forth.

Wedding planning tends to reveal people's true personality. For example, a person who is an impulsive spender will find it difficult to work with the wedding budget and will show traits of being inconsiderate when spending uncontrollably. I have seen couples who have decided to call it quits during their wedding planning process as a result of what they discovered about each other's personalities.

At this stage, you learn how to make decisions together, learn to prioritize each other, and how to plan your schedule together if you've not been doing that prior to getting engaged. This is to show you that the work never stops. You must continue to work on yourself as an individual and as a couple together.

Chapter Ten Questions

1.   What is your major takeaway from this chapter?

2.   How do you plan to apply what you've learned in this phase to your relationship now or in the future?

3.   How do you plan to continue to build and grow your relationship through this phase?

4.   How do you plan to make sure your wedding planning or transitioning phase is about you and your partner and not you alone?

5.   What is your mindset about compromise? How do you plan to make room for this in the transitioning phase?

6.   How has this chapter prepared your mind for transition into marriage?

CONCLUSION

In conclusion, this book has covered the steps to be taken toward finding your God-given partner while applying biblical principles. We've established the fact that it should all start with God as it is written in Matthew 22:37-39, that there are two great commandments: "To love the Lord your God with all your heart, soul, and mind and the second is like it, to love your neighbor as yourself." This essentially means to first, love God and secondly love your neighborhood as you love yourself as I believe the love of God in your heart will make it possible for you to fulfill this.

Therefore, if everyone is doing their part as Christians in following these principles, it will not be difficult to love and be loved in return. Let it be engraved in your heart that God is the love you seek and the love you seek in human beings does not exist without God being involved. Finally, be intentional about finding your God-given partner while holding on to your Christian values and principles. Remember, marriage is not a destination. We are all journeying through life and identifying someone to do this with is not to be taken with levity.

Thank you for reading this book. I hope you have been blessed and have viewed dating and courtship through a spiritual lens. I hope this book creates a desire to approach the process of finding your God-given partner with all seriousness in surrender to God. I strongly believe in the Word in Philippians 4:19, *"But my God shall supply all your needs according to his riches in glory by Christ Jesus."* This scripture is applicable both to the need for a wife or a husband.

While the content of this book serves as a guide, I submit and acknowledge that God is the ultimate guide we need. His Word is a lamp unto our feet and light to our path (Psalm 119:105). I encourage you to spend time studying the Word of God and some of the scriptures referenced in this book. I pray that the Spirit of God will direct your path and guide you to choose the right life partner whom He has crafted especially for you.

ABOUT THE AUTHOR

Funke Oladele is a healthcare professional, motivator, public speaker and purpose activator. She is the founder of Beyond Africa Magazine and the host of the BAM podcast, a success inspiration platform. Funke's passion and purpose is focused on success inspiration and dating/relationships, empowering people to maximize their potentials while building healthy relationships. Her professional career is focused on quality/process improvement (Lean Six Sigma) and project management.

Funke is married to Seun Oladele, a Gospel Artist, and they are blessed with two beautiful girls.

She has been privileged to serve as a youth and young adult group leader for about ten years. In this role, she has had the opportunity to present and coach on dating and relationships at youth conferences, small singles group settings, and one-on-one meetings.

Funke has always dreamed of becoming an author and has spent many years using her writings to provide inspiration and enlightenment. She started her first blog www.inkatheart.wordpress.com which was based on life, love and relationships.

Funke Oladele is available for coaching, webinars, and conferences on topics such as goal setting, purpose, dating and relationships.

Visit www.funkeoladele.com to learn more about the Author

Email: Info@funkeoladele.com

Instagram: @Funkeeoladele

BOOK REVIEWS

This book is perfect for those who struggle having a healthy Christian relationship. It provides great advice and speaks the truth about how to be successful in your relationship. As a single woman, I've spent my entire life trying to do relationships my own way or in accordance with social media's standards. And now thanks to this book, I am able to see more clearly God's way to engage in a relationship.

~Elizabeth Akinrinsola

A must read for young women and men considering dating and marriage. Biblically based advice! Youth leaders and church school leaders, and parents: Read this! Give it to your teens! Talk about it with them! It will be well worth the time spent.

~Margaret Beasley

In a world with so much emphasis on self: self-love, self-help and even being in a relationship with oneself, ***Finding Your God-Given Partner*** *takes one on a journey from focus on self, to focus on fulfilling God's purpose through finding and maintaining that relationship that not only honors God, but brings peace and joy to the one who finds it. It is a manual that is certified to result in success—beginning from the very start: dating—all the way to marriage. It lays a solid foundation regarding this complex topic of dating in regard to relationships and continues on with arranging the success blocks that will guarantee that dating results* *in courtship and will eventually result in marriage. While the book is aimed at young Christian singles—gently admonishing them to avoid relationship pitfalls and encouraging them on the not-so-mainstream notions such as waiting on God and defining one's identity before jumping into a relationship. I also strongly recommend this book for married Christians as it captures the essence of what makes marriages thrive such as the importance of clear communication in regard to goals and expectations. For example, how many kids, how to handle finances; what kind of life is desired—and even more importantly, the principle of mutual spiritual growth. Funke captures timeless biblical truths, and her tone is clear on its gentle inclusivity, cutting across cultural and demographical barriers. She is very effective at her attempt to reveal Godly concepts through practical and secular tips such that even a non-Christian will understand the hows, and whats and whys to ensure they find themselves in a relationship that will effectively graduate to a happy marriage.*

~Olubunmi Akindebe

Made in the USA
Middletown, DE
05 November 2022

14085863R00086